Young Pathfinder 12

Working together

*O*ther titles in the **Young Pathfinder** *series*

CiLT The National Centre for Languages

CILT, the National Centre for Languages, seeks to support and develop multilingualism and intercultural competence among all sectors of the population in the UK.

CILT serves education, business and the wider community with:
- specialised and impartial information services;
- high quality advice and professional development;
- expert support for innovation and development;
- quality improvement in language skills and service provision.

CILT is a charitable trust, supported by the DfES and other Government departments throughout the UK.

early language learning

ELL is a DfES initiative managed by CILT, the National Centre for Languages, working in partnership with QCA, BECTA, the British Council Education and Training Group, the TTA, OFSTED and the Association for Language Learning.

Young Pathfinder 12

A CILT series for primary language teachers

Working together

Native speaker assistants in the primary school

Cynthia Martin and Anne Farren

The views expressed in this publication are the authors' and do not necessarily represent those of CILT.

Acknowledgements

Cynthia Martin would like to thank all teachers and native speakers with whom she has worked in primary languages projects over the years and especially Lucy Adamson, Christine Allan, Sophie Baus, Pat Bertaux, Jo Biddle, Ann Brooks, Andy Burford, Jo Cole, Anne Dareys, Mina Drever, Phil Farrar, Virginia Hill, Kathleen Manley, Nigel Pearson, Andrew Portas, Anita Rowell, Glynis Rumley, Richard Smith, Alison Taylor. She would also like to thank Bill Musk and Joan Hoggan from the British Council and Hugh Baldry and Peter Fairbrace from the Teacher Training Agency. Anne Farren would like to thank teachers and native speaker assistants from Richmond upon Thames for their invaluable contributions.

First published 2004 by CILT, the National Centre for Languages, 20 Bedfordbury, London WC2N 4LB

Copyright © CILT 2004

ISBN 1 904243 31 2

A catalogue record for this book is available from the British Library

Series cover design by Neil Alexander
Photography (cover and page 64) © 2004 Barbara Ludman/iwitness

Printed in Great Britain by Hobbs

CILT Publications are available from: **Central Books**, 99 Wallis Rd, London E9 5LN. Tel: 0845 458 9910. Fax: 0845 458 9912. Book trade representation (UK and Ireland): **Broadcast Book Services**, Charter House, 29a London Rd, Croydon CR0 2RE. Tel: 020 8681 8949. Fax: 020 8688 0615.

Contents

Introduction: Towards entitlement

The *National Languages Strategy: Languages for all, Languages for life* (DfES 2002) proposes that by 2010 all pupils from the age of seven will be entitled to learn a foreign language in primary school. With some 20,000 primary schools across England, many creative approaches are being found to deliver this entitlement. One of these involves the deployment of native speakers, to which the National Languages Strategy makes several references:

> *Every child should have the opportunity throughout Key Stage 2 to study a foreign language and develop their interest in the culture of other nations. They should have access to high quality teaching and learning opportunities, making use of native speakers and e-learning.* (DfES 2002: 15)

> *Numbers of language assistants in primary schools will increase and training will be targeted to ensure that they can play a meaningful role in helping to teach languages.* (DfES 2002: 32)

Before this, the *Nuffield Languages Inquiry Report* recommended that:

> *primary schools should be offered incentives to recruit Foreign Language Assistants as classroom helpers.* (Nuffield Foundation 2000: 43)

Nearly a decade earlier, the National Association of Head Teachers proposed that:

> *the Government be called upon to promote and support [...] the increased provision of Foreign Language Assistants to facilitate the introduction of foreign language teaching into primary schools.* (NAHT Resolution 19 May 1992)

So we can see that the idea of deploying native speaker assistants in the primary school is not a new one. Since the mid 1990s there has been an increasing pool of experience upon which to draw, as more and more native speaker assistants are working in primary schools. How best can we maximise their potential and ensure that **both** the native speakers **and** their host schools get the very best out of any arrangements that are made? *Working together* aims to provide practical support to primary schools introducing languages into the curriculum and considering working with a native speaker in order to deliver the Languages Strategy entitlement. It starts by offering some reasons why you might wish to collaborate with a native speaker to enhance your primary languages programme and highlights some of the benefits to be gained from working with native speakers in the primary school. The book is divided into eight chapters, each of which draws on the experiences of a range of colleagues and includes a number of practical tips to help you make a success of working with a native speaker assistant. These tips are highlighted throughout the book for ease of reference.

- Chapter 1 presents a rationale for working with native speaker assistants and indicates some of the potential benefits.
- Chapter 2 considers practical organisational issues such as different ways of finding a native speaker to support primary languages work, signalling sources of further information.
- Chapter 3 focuses on different models for ways of organising and timetabling native speakers.
- In Chapter 4 we offer some guidelines for Local Education Authorities (LEAs), higher education institutions and secondary schools working with primary schools and native speakers.
- Chapter 5 is addressed to primary teachers preparing for a native speaker appointment.
- Chapter 6 offers some suggestions for supporting the native speaker, both on arrival and throughout their period in primary school.
- Chapter 7 includes some examples of the ways in which native speakers have been used to enhance primary languages work.
- Chapter 8 considers ways of building on the work of the native speaker.

All chapters draw on the experiences of colleagues working in a variety of educational contexts, such as LEAs, higher education institutions involved in teacher training, Specialist Language Colleges, secondary and primary schools and, of course, we have reflections from native speakers and children too.

1. Why use a native speaker assistant?

This chapter considers the potential benefits to be gained from using a well-supported native speaker assistant. As we shall see from the examples below, it is not only the children but also their teachers who gain from the additional person in the classroom. This chapter therefore begins by presenting factors for teachers to consider, listing some of the ways in which a native speaker may be able to support the primary class teacher, whether it be linguistically, culturally, or professionally. We then indicate how inviting native speakers into the primary classroom can help develop children's interest in and positive attitude towards different countries and cultures, as well as developing a whole range of skills. Throughout, we incorporate some of the views and experiences of teachers who have worked with a variety of native speakers. St Bede's RC Comprehensive School, a Specialist Language College in Lanchester has discovered: 'Primaries hugely value native speakers.' Some of the reasons are given below.

Primary teachers whose schools are only just beginning the process of introducing a language to pupils in readiness for 2010, may be wondering if their foreign language knowledge and skills are up to the task. Perhaps you are feeling anxious about your pronunciation and intonation, or whether your knowledge of both the language and the culture of the target language country are sufficiently up to date. You will find that if you plan carefully and script a limited amount of target language which you intend to use, starting small and gradually building up your repertoire as you reuse specific phrases for classroom routines, simple instructions and praise, you will be able to sustain quite a bit of target language in your lessons. (For hints about ways of teaching through the target language see Young Pathfinder 5: *Keep talking: Teaching in the target language* (Satchwell 1997)). Of course, you will also need additional linguistic support which is available through many excellent published resources such as the interactive CD-ROMS, *Pilote moi* and *Mon école* (Kent Educational Television 1995), or the videos which accompany the Early Start French and Spanish materials and the *3,2,1 los* German videos (Early Start Languages). In these resources, 'virtual' native speakers, both adults and children, can be seen and heard talking about their daily lives. Most of these resources contain additional sections, CDs or audio-cassettes which offer examples of classroom language and its pronunciation for teachers.

In addition, you may be fortunate in having a secondary specialist who can help deliver some of the language lessons as a training opportunity, demonstrating ways of incorporating plenty of mime, gesture and facial expression to make the target language clearer to learners. If you can involve parents or other language speaking adults from the school community or share a native speaker from a nearby secondary school, further expertise can be tapped into. Don't forget that the native speaker assistants will also appreciate seeing **you** in action with your class, especially when you are teaching literacy and numeracy, or using storybooks.

To sum up, we can say that, for teachers, a native speaker working closely with class teachers can complement the above kinds of resources and be a source of linguistic support. This is especially the case for teachers who are not confident in the language and who need some additional reassurance about various aspects of the foreign language. For example, the native speaker can help by:

- providing an excellent model of pronunciation – a vital requirement as we know that young children are capable of imitating with great accuracy;
- helping with the target language.

One class teacher explains, 'Our native speaker was like a "living dictionary", able to supply colleagues with the latest colloquial expressions, equivalents of "great, cool, wicked"'.

The native speaker can also support the primary teacher by acting as a partner in dialogues, taking part in question and answer sequences and helping to model games and pairwork activities. This latter role is important as it demonstrates foreign language interaction between two adult speakers for a real purpose and is different from whole class presentation of new language items by the class teacher on his or her own. This does, of course, mean that the **class teacher must remain in the room with the native speaker assistant** and be prepared to participate!

The video and CD materials mentioned earlier in this chapter, also feature examples of different festivals and celebrations from the target-language countries. These will help contribute to work in citizenship and develop both your pupils' and your own cultural understanding. Typically, the participants in the videos and CD-ROMs are not actors, but children and local inhabitants going about their daily lives, with their homes, schools, villages and towns in the background. If you have not had the opportunity to visit the target-language country for a while, having access to a native speaker can support the intercultural strand of the Key Stage 2 Framework for Languages (see also **www.cilt.org.uk/cpd/primary.htm** for information on how to participate in training events at home and abroad). We may therefore say that, for teachers, native speakers can not only be a source of cultural input, but they can also assist the teacher by:

- updating teachers' knowledge of customs and festivals;
- being a source of authentic materials (CDs, songs, photos, poems, posters, pictures, digital camera clips, etc);
- talking about the foreign language culture and way of life with specialised local and national knowledge.

Native speakers can also contribute to classroom management by being an extra pair of hands, eyes or ears when children need additional support and monitoring during pairwork, games or other activities. Finally, they also contribute to the professional development of teachers by:

- giving non-specialist teachers confidence to carry on with activities they have introduced;
- developing teachers' understanding of other school systems and approaches;
- updating teachers' knowledge of the foreign language;
- giving teachers fresh ideas.

In the words of a primary languages co-ordinator from The Queen's C.E. Primary School, Kew: 'Cécile, teaching the Year 4 classes, gave teachers the chance to observe and get ideas'.

Nigel Pearson

If you have had the opportunity to use some of the video or CD-based materials mentioned earlier in this chapter, you will find that having watched children in the target-language country, pupils are keen to communicate with 'real' foreign language speakers. This is where having access to a native speaker can be so enriching, not only for teachers but also for pupils, for whom there are many benefits, too. The next section summarises some of the reasons why. As Nigel Pearson from Liverpool LEA says, 'Young native speakers can represent a teacher from a different generation.' As a result, native speakers can both help motivate and excite the learners and make learning more purposeful and relevant. This is what the French Co-ordinator at Clarendon School, Hampton has to say:

Our French assistant has had a great impact on raising the profile of languages in the school. Pupils all enjoy lessons and motivation is improved. They can see the relevance of learning a language, having met a 'real, live' French person.

In addition to all of this, the native speaker can extend the range of target language sources to be listened to and help develop more focused listening skills. As the Headteacher of Lowther Primary School in Barnes reflects: 'Having a native speaker raises the skill of listening for all ages'.

Indeed, growth in self esteem and other skills is not limited to older primary pupils, but children in early years and foundation stage settings can derive great benefit from a native speaker too, developing children's communicative skills. A native speaker assistant in the primary classroom can also provide an accurate and authentic model of spoken language for children to copy, and interact with children in speaking tasks when teaching a song or reading a story. As one nursery teacher from Richmond upon Thames points out:

*The children gained confidence in trying to copy without any inhibitions. Their **listening skills** improved, as they had to 'tune into' new speech patterns. Their **observational skills** were also enhanced as they looked at gestures and visual aids for clues to meaning.*

The above comments indicate the way in which working together with a native speaker assistant can help develop children's oracy skills and thus address one of the strands of the Key Stage 2 Framework for MFL, which will be introduced nationally in 2005. In addition, their contribution can help provide enjoyment for both teachers and children, creating enthusiastic learners with positive attitudes. As a Year 2 Berkshire teacher explains:

*The children have benefited enormously. They have greatly enjoyed the sessions, learnt a lot about the language and the culture, which they **remember** and have developed strong enthusiasm for learning languages.*

The National Languages Strategy makes the point that 'language competence and intercultural understanding are not optional extras, they are an essential part of being a citizen' (DfES 2002: 5). If a class teacher is aiming to create a classroom environment which exposes children to both the language and the **culture** of the target language country, encouraging empathy for and curiosity about the country and its people, then from a cultural perspective, native speakers can:

- enable children to get used to meeting people from other countries;
- generate a genuine interest in foreign peoples and their cultures;
- introduce or reinforce the European and international dimensions;
- provide a real link with the country where the foreign language is spoken.

Another class teacher suggests: 'These children should go on with a positive attitude to speaking other languages and an acceptance of similarities and differences between cultures'.

If the activities focus on looking afresh at the home community, manners and customs, starting with children's own experiences and exploring similarities and differences between their own lives and those of their counterparts in the target-language countries, having a native speaker assistant, even for a short time, can have a real impact. As one teacher from Berkshire tells us: 'The children have benefited in a growth of confidence, tolerance of others, respect for other ways of doing things as well as learning a little of the languages'.

Jo Cole, from South Gloucestershire, says of the French assistant who works in the local cluser of schools: 'Children gain a lot of knowledge and understanding by working with a "real" French person'. And a Year 4 pupil from Hampshire talking about the Foreign Language Assistant who worked in their primary school, explains: 'I like it because **she's really French**'.

The additional person in the languages classroom can also:

- be a means to offer the foreign language to smaller groups either to support or extend pupils;
- help by giving valuable individual attention;
- support late starters, pupils returning after absence, newcomers to the class who need to catch up;
- offer further challenge to gifted and talented pupils;
- extend pupils who speak the language at home.

Jo Cole

One junior school teacher in Richmond upon Thames enthuses:

The children looked forward to working with Ariane, who was always incredibly enthusiastic – the fact that she was always smiles and so positive, meant that she brought a breath of fresh air to our staffroom.

The Headteacher of Heathfield Infant and Nursery School in Whitton says: 'Isabelle was delightful with the children. She gave them an excellent mixture of learning and fun; they were all very proud of their new skill!'.

Indeed, as Nigel Pearson points out, 'People are the main resource in primary languages teaching and learning'.

● ● ● ● ●

Your school will only get the best out of native speaker assistants, whoever they may be, if the ground is thoroughly prepared and their contribution is planned and supported. You will find that very strong partnerships can be formed when a specialist teacher, primary teacher **and** native speaker assistant participate together in teaching and learning activities in the classroom. We will go on to explore these issues in Chapters 4, 5 and 6.

> Ce stage a été pour moi une expérience enrichissante me permettant de découvrir un autre système éducatif, une autre méthode d'enseignement du français.
>
> *This placement has been an enriching experience, that has enabled me to discover a different education system and way of teaching French.* (Catherine, newly qualified teacher from Paris)

> *This three weeks has been a very enriching experience. The organisation was efficient from the first day (timetable, room), and the lessons were interesting both for the children and me. I think that it is necessary to encourage such internships. The use of E-learning is a very good way to work within a network of French and English schools, and to create innovative partnerships between our two countries.* (Olivier, newly qualified teacher from Paris)

2. Finding your native speaker assistant

DIFFERENT TYPES OF NATIVE SPEAKER ASSISTANT

Broadly speaking, native speaker assistants in the primary school classroom fall into four categories. They may be:

- Foreign Language Assistants;
- Comenius Language Assistants;
- trainee teachers from abroad – either participating in the DfES/Teacher Training Agency Initial Teacher Training Primary Languages Project or in LEA co-ordinated schemes;
- native speakers from within the local community.

FOREIGN LANGUAGE ASSISTANTS

Foreign Language Assistants are typically young native speakers, often undergraduates or recent graduates. They are usually interested in coming to England in order to improve their English, which they may be studying at university in their home country. Some may be intending to teach later on but, generally, they do **not** have a teacher training background and only very rarely are they already trained teachers. They will therefore require specific support and guidance in order to teach effectively (see Chapters 5 and 6). The table below gives an outline of what is involved in employing a Foreign Language Assistant.

Foreign Language Assistants who are going to work in a maintained primary or secondary school	need to be appointed through the LEA, in liaison with the British Council Education and Training Group
Period in the UK	usually 1 October to 31 May (8 months)
Teach	12 hours a week (this can be extended by mutual agreement if additional pro-rata payments are made)
Attachment	to a primary school, or shared between a primary and secondary school, or between primary schools
Role	**mainly linguistic**
Cost (2004/05)	£5,896 (exclusive National Insurance and London Allowance)
Cost met by	host school(s), or where appropriate, LEA
Deadline for applications	check with LEA
To find out more	go to **www.languageassistant.co.uk** and **assistants@britishcouncil.org**

As can be seen from the above, assistants can be appointed by the LEA to work on a peripatetic basis, usually in a maximum of three schools, unless the scheme is very well established with extremely high quality support. The employing institution, at a rate set each year by the DfES, meets their salary. As an example, for the year 2004/05, this works out at £5,896 (exclusive of National Insurance and the London Allowance). Schools should check with their LEA about the deadline for expressions of interest.

COMENIUS LANGUAGE ASSISTANTS

The Comenius Language Assistant programme (formerly Lingua Action C) is funded by the European Union to promote the teaching and learning of foreign languages and to strengthen the European dimension in the curriculum. It is part of SOCRATES, the EU education programme and will be in place until 2006. Keep an eye on the British Council's website for details of the programme after this period: **www.britishcouncil.org.uk**.

Comenius Language Assistants	can help support a European Educational Partnership/Comenius project
Period in the UK	minimum of three months – maximum eight months; Comenius language assistants can decide how long they want the placement to be and when they wish to start. Normally this is between 1 September and 30 June
Teach	12–16 hours a week, maximum 18
Attachment	in up to three different schools
Role	**to help develop the international dimension: cultural as well as linguistic input**
Cost (2004/05)	receive a monthly allowance as well as their return travel expenses to the UK
Cost met by	Comenius Assistants' national agency (no cost to the host primary school); only cost incurred by the host school is travel to a briefing meeting held for host school co-ordinators at the British Council
Deadline for applications	1 February
To find out more	go to **www.socrates-uk.net/comenius**

The Comenius Language Assistant programme allows prospective language teachers to spend time in schools across Europe to work as teaching assistants. It is particularly relevant for native speakers who are actively considering teaching and the majority of participants have completed at least two years' study at higher education level providing access to a career as a teacher. Currently some 30 countries are involved in the Comenius Programme.

There is, however, no guarantee that a host school will be allocated a Comenius Assistant from a particular country, although efforts are made to match the school and assistants according to the preferences they have expressed. The main benefit a Comenius Assistant will bring to your primary school is an authentic presence from another European country.

Comenius Language Assistants must spend some time teaching their native language and the programme is keen to promote the less widely taught languages of the European Union, such as Swedish. Hosting a Comenius Language Assistant can be a means of introducing your pupils to other European cultures, languages and perspectives, by offering your school the opportunity to find out about countries and languages other than France, Germany and Spain. Naturally however, Comenius Assistants from these countries do take part in the scheme. In addition, Comenius Language Assistants also work across the curriculum in other subject areas such as art and music.

Although Foreign Language Assistants and Comenius Assistants meet their own accommodation costs, it is usual for the host institution to help them find somewhere to live, at least in the first instance.

 You can share a Comenius Language Assistant with up to two other schools by putting in a joint application. One of the three schools should make the application to the British Council on behalf of the other(s).

TRAINEE TEACHERS FROM OTHER EUROPEAN COUNTRIES

A third category of native speaker is the growing number of **teacher trainees** from other countries in mainland Europe spending four weeks on school-based exchange placements in England. Many of these trainees will be participating in the ITT Primary Languages Project launched in autumn 2001 and being managed on behalf of the DfES by the Teacher Training Agency. They may be from a French IUFM (*Institut Universitaire de Formation des Maîtres*), from a German *Pädagogische Hochschule*, from a university in Spain or, from 2004, teachers from Italy and, from 2005, from teacher training institutions in Portugal.

For these trainee teachers, the placement in an English primary school is an integral part of their initial teacher training programme. Unlike Foreign Language Assistants, who are engaged mainly in teaching their own language, these trainee teachers, in addition to teaching their mother tongue, will want to teach as much as possible using **English**. There will also be a requirement that they teach a range of subjects across the primary curriculum. While they are in your school they will be visited by tutors from the host teacher training institution in England and perhaps, additionally, by tutors from their home country.

Initial teacher trainees	will be available through your local higher education institution
Period in the UK	four weeks at any time during the school year
Teach	a programme tailored to their own and the primary school's needs including some whole class teaching
Attachment	to a single primary school usually in partnership with the higher education institution
Role	**linguistic (teaching their mother tongue) and cross curricular – using English to teach elements of the primary curriculum**
Cost (2004/05)	none to host primary schools
Cost met by	higher education institution, funded by the Teacher Training Agency
Deadline for applications	by mutual agreement with higher education institution
To find out more	go to **www.langprim.org**

Where LEAs have links with higher education institutions abroad, locally arranged programmes might exist, such as in Richmond upon Thames. For further details about how a scheme linking an LEA with teacher training institutions from abroad might work, see Chapter 3. The following is an extract from a letter inviting schools to host a trainee teacher from Spain.

Dear Colleague,

Placements for trainee teachers from Spain

You are invited to participate in next year's programme in which Richmond is playing host to colleagues from Barcelona for the second time.

The aim of this initiative is twofold. Your school will benefit from having a Spanish visitor in school who can introduce some language teaching and contribute a European dimension to a variety of curriculum areas. They are also able to act as a general classroom assistant. In return, your visitor will experience life in an English primary school and have the opportunity to develop their command of English classroom language.

Visitors often have particular expertise or interests that they are willing to contribute, such as cookery, festivals and traditions, arts or history and geography.

In South Gloucestershire, Jo Cole notes:

> *Trainees give 'free' support, which is much appreciated by the primary heads and teachers.*

NATIVE SPEAKERS FROM WITHIN THE LOCAL COMMUNITY

Last, but by no means least, there are **native speakers living in the local community** – parents, governors or neighbours perhaps, who have skills which enable them to support foreign language teaching in primary schools. As the National Languages Strategy states:

> *As part of the broader strategy to remodel the school workforce, adults with language skills, such as native speakers, people within the community and those in business will be encouraged to work with teachers to deliver language learning at Key Stage 2.* (DfES 2002: 31)

Glynis Rumley from Kent has had substantial experience deploying native speakers from within the local community. The majority of these native speakers have been French mothers, who had either been in contact with the primary school in which they later worked, or who were recommended by primary schools. Glynis highlights some of the organisational advantages, which can come from using native speakers who are local to the host primary school. For example:

- many have their own cars and can get around between the primary schools in which they work more easily than Foreign Language Assistants, who do not always have their own transport;
- they have their own home, so there are no accommodation issues.

Another advantage of this type of local native speaker is that as most are resident in the county, with children in local schools, they are already familiar with the English school system and have absorbed a good deal of English culture. Even more importantly, if they are mothers, this helps them understand primary aged children and most are good at adapting their own children's games and songs to help them teach in school.

Furthermore, a major asset is the supportive infrastructure of which they are already a part: usually settled and comfortable in the UK with English friends.

In Liverpool, the LEA receives many employment enquiries from native speakers already resident in the local area, or with friends who are working there, and reports that they usually adapt more quickly to teaching because they are settled and aware of local conditions. Nigel Pearson sums up their contribution for us:

- these helpers vary in age and make a very valuable contribution to that extra dimension in language learning;
- when working with the native speaker assistants in the classroom, the MFL specialist teacher uses the target language when speaking to them and this enables the children to encounter another authentic language source communicating for real purposes;

- with the native speaker, the teacher can model conversations or demonstrate games and thus there is no need for explanations in English as the children quickly learn by observing what is expected;
- the native speakers and helpers frequently travel to a German-speaking country for family visits or holidays and they can then provide authentic resources to support learning, including comics and magazines, a *Schultüte* (a bag of goodies for pupils on their first day school), a *Hampelmann* (puppet) and certain foods;
- some native speakers are 'in the know' as to whom to approach for sponsorship, say for a languages event.

The following table summarises some of the characteristics of native speakers from the community.

Native speakers from within the community	likely to be available through local networks
Period in the UK	throughout the school year, although perhaps not full time but on specific days each week
Teach	by mutual arrangement with the host primary school
Attachment	to one or more primary schools as suits local circumstances
Role	**to support the delivery of primary languages**
Cost	negotiated on a school-by-school basis, in some cases they may volunteer
Cost met by	host primary school(s) – employment legislation means that schools rather than the LEA are now encouraged to employ native speakers in this category directly
To find out more	your LEA may be able to provide advice; this must include vetting by the Criminal Records Bureau

It is important to bear in mind that since native speakers from the local community may *not* be part of a structured programme, training will not necessarily be immediately available from external sources and support must be provided.

Furthermore, despite being native speakers and even where they already have a primary teaching qualification from their own country, they may not have had any experience of *teaching their own language*, which raises new challenges for host primary schools.

Andy Burford, headteacher at Liss Junior School, reports that their native speaker assistant from the local community found it really helpful to have access to teaching materials provided by the school, for example the QCA schemes of work for Key Stage 2 and other publications, containing songs and structured lesson plans as exemplars. This was the case, even though the native speaker had previously qualified as a primary teacher in France. Of course, all native speaker assistants will appreciate access to support materials to help with planning.

Some of these native speakers from within the local community may be employed as teaching assistants (TAs) or higher level teaching assistants (HLTAs) for whom training programmes are currently being developed. From September 2005, native speakers within the local community will have the opportunity to follow a 20-hour course for teaching assistants that will be offered as a stand-alone or as part of a higher level teaching assistant course. Information can be obtained from the Teacher Training Agency.

● ● ● ● ●

This chapter has outlined some of the different ways you may be able to gain the support of a native speaker assistant for your primary languages programme. Chapter 3 offers some suggestions for organising the deployment of native speaker assistants.

3. Deploying your native speaker assistant

This chapter considers organisational issues relating to the deployment of native speakers. As you can see from the preceding chapter, the number of hours native speakers will be available to an individual school is likely to depend on several factors, such as the overall length and purpose of their stay in the UK and whether they are attached to a single primary school for the duration of their placement, shared between several primary schools, or between a primary and associated secondary school. A whole variety of practice is therefore possible. Native speakers may work in a primary school for the better part of the school year, for a whole or half a term, a month or even less.

The following section shows different ways it is possible for an LEA to organise the deployment of native speakers, bearing in mind contact time of between 12 and 16 hours each. Careful co-ordination and a high level of support are paramount.

A LOCAL EDUCATION AUTHORITY PERSPECTIVE

Foreign Language Assistants have been deployed in the London Borough of Richmond upon Thames LEA primary and special schools since 1993. The extent of the provision on offer is dependent upon the funding available in any given year. At the time of writing, this is organised as follows.

Option A	Option B	Option C
Schools subscribe to a service level agreement (£625 per year). This entitles them to 27 hours of Foreign Language Assistant input, which equates to three hours a week over a nine-week period.	Key Stage 2 MFL Pathfinder funding enables similar blocks of time to be allocated to non-subscribing schools.	Schools combine options A and B and receive 54 hours of Foreign Language Assistant time over an eighteen-week period.

The Foreign Language Assistant provision described above would typically be available between 1 October and 31 May. The LEA takes responsibility for finding accommodation and overall line management of the assistants.

Where, as in this case, a small team of assistants serves several primary schools, the timetable allows them to work for a block of time in four schools, on set days each week, Monday to Thursday, transferring at the end of the 'block' to another group of schools. This gives an element of stability despite the change of schools at the end of each block.

An illustration of how this might work:

Block 1 6 October – 11 December	Monday	Tuesday	Wednesday	Thursday
Isabelle	St Joseph's	Hampton Court	Kew Gardens	Forge Green
Doris	Richmond Park	Kingston Road	St John's	Heathcote
Stéphanie	The Orchard	Holy Cross	Green Lanes	St Mary's
Patricia	Middlegate	Denton	Chandler Court	Ember Bridge

Block 2 5 January – 11 March	Monday	Tuesday	Wednesday	Thursday
Isabelle	Greer House	Hampton Court	Kew Gardens	Percy Road
Doris	Richmond Park	Kingston Road	Kingwood	Heathcote
Stéphanie	The Orchard	The Avenue	Green Lanes	St Mary's
Patricia	Middlegate	St Elizabeth's	Chandler Court	St Paul's

 If possible, try to avoid a change of school during the same school day. If you are organising on behalf of an LEA or Specialist Language College, for example, try to use schools that are close together. If you are working within a family or cluster of primary schools, perhaps you can organise the programme in such a way that transport problems are avoided. This may be more difficult in rural locations where primary schools are more spread out.

All 160 primary schools in Liverpool have access to native speakers. A team of 19 Foreign Language Assistants currently delivers French, Spanish and German to pupils on a weekly basis in up to 10 schools each, while Arabic will be introduced shortly into four primaries as part of the Key Stage 2 Pathfinder project. This established project involves specialist language teachers working with well supported Foreign Language Assistants, complemented in some instances by input on one day a week from a native speaker from the local community. In Liverpool prime responsibility for delivery of the foreign language is undertaken by MFL specialist teachers and the native speakers work alongside the specialist, team teaching and focusing on group work to target slower learners or high fliers. This is especially the case with the Centres of Excellence for Spanish, French and German.

NATIVE SPEAKER TRAINEE TEACHERS FROM ABROAD

Richmond upon Thames is an example of a local education authority that hosts native speaker teacher trainees via two different schemes. In the first scheme, the Foreign Language Assistant provision is complemented by LEA co-ordinated placements of Spanish trainee teachers who arrive for one month in September. They are allocated one host school and work a full teaching week. A partnership agreement between their university and the LEA means that this is now recognised as an official teaching practice. When funding permits, their university tutor visits the students and this has helped build up a relationship with the schools. This year, the LEA adviser was able to attend a briefing meeting in Spain prior to the students' departure and, again, this was effective in preparing them for their placement.

Under the second scheme, visiting French teachers, at the end of their training course at the IUFM de Créteil, arrive in June of each year for one month. They work a fifteen-hour week and some schools involve them in school journeys and activities weeks. Where schools have the capacity to do so, they host two or even three visitors and this enables team teaching or coverage of a wider spread of pupils.

Host schools are required to **find, but not fund**, accommodation for the visitors and this is usually in the home of a teacher or parents. Guidelines outlining the responsibilities of all those involved are given out (see overleaf).

Under a third scheme currently around 30 higher education institutions are participating in the DfES/TTA Initial Teacher Training Primary Languages Project (see **www.langprim.org**). Some of these providers offer primary languages training as part of the one-year postgraduate certificate in education route, while others do so as part of a three- or four-year undergraduate programme leading to a BEd or BA (QTS). This is a shared initiative between the Teacher Training Agency in England, the Ministère de l'Education in France, the Baden-Württemberg, Berlin and Nordrhein Westfalen governments in Germany, the Ministerio de Educación in Spain and teacher training institutions in Italy and Portugal. Under the auspices of this project, each higher education institution has been partnered with a teacher training institution in partner countries, allowing not only an exchange of ideas but of personnel. As a result, native speaker teacher trainees are required to spend a month in a primary school in their partner country. During this time they may be visited by tutors from the higher education institution's partner institution in the target language country.

Guidelines for schools receiving native speaker trainees under an LEA scheme

Placement of trainee teachers from Spain • 15 September–10 October 2003

Aims of the placement
To participate in the life of an English primary school for 15 hours a week, contributing to the teaching of language and culture and acting as a general classroom helper.

Responsibilities of the LEA
- To co-ordinate the school placements.
- To act as a link between the university and the schools.
- To offer advice and support to schools on planning and organisation.
- To provide induction and debriefing sessions for the visitors and at least one meeting half way through the placement.

Responsibilities of the school
- To find accommodation for the visitor, preferably somewhere near the school and to act as a point of contact with the host family.
- To identify a host teacher who will be the main point of contact; it is helpful if this is someone who is there every day.
- To prepare a programme for the first few days that will allow opportunities to meet the staff and pupils, and to observe some teaching.
- To prepare a timetable, so that the visitor is clear about their daily activities.
- To include the visitor in any activities, such as school journeys, where this is appropriate.
- To accommodate by agreement, any particular subject interests that the visitor might have (such as dance, cookery, painting or music).
- To provide a school lunch if desired.

Responsibilities of the host family
- To provide accommodation, on a room only basis, but with access to cooking facilities, for £70 a week.
- To negotiate prior to the visitor's arrival, any changes to the above arrangement (i.e. a lower rate in exchange for language tuition or babysitting; a higher rate to include meals).
- To arrange with the visitor, the time and place of their arrival (i.e. at a local train or tube station).
- To liaise with the host school should any issues arise.

Responsibilities of the trainee teacher
- To make initial contact with the host school and identify what materials it would be useful to bring (e.g. photos) and to discuss any school subject interests.
- To make initial contact wih the host family to make arrangements about time of arrival and the nearest train or tube station.
- To participate fully in the life of the school and to agree any changes to the programme with the host teacher.
- To liaise with the host teacher if any issues arise.

Many thanks to all the visitors, schools and host families, without whom this scheme would not be possible.

Under the DfES/TTA scheme, native speaker teacher trainees arrive in England to take up their four-week exchange placement throughout the school year and precisely when they do so, will depend on the arrangements made between each higher education institution and its partner training provider abroad. Negotiating a suitable set of dates for the exchange placements to take place can be complex and in some instances higher education institutions and their partners may try out several different times over successive years, as their programmes evolve. This means that primary schools will not necessarily receive trainees at the same time each succeeding year, until the programmes have bedded down. The first decision will, however, involve mutually agreeing with the partner in the target language country on an appropriate point in the academic year for the exchange to occur. According to when this is, the weight attached to the placement by the sending institution will have to be checked, for example:

- Is the placement taking place early on in the academic year and therefore **formative** in role?
- Does it **replace** a **key teaching placement** in the home country?
- Do the native speakers require a particular **Key Stage** during their time in the UK?
- Does it require a **minimum number of teaching hours?**
- Will the native speaker trainees have **specific tasks** set by their home institution to complete?
- Will **summative** assessment at the end be necessary, with grades that 'count' towards qualified teacher status in the sending country?

In France, for instance, nursery and primary schooling is organised in three *cycles*: Primary school *(Ecole primaire)* is divided into two sections, the *Ecole Maternelle* and the *Ecole Elémentaire*. *Cycle 1* covers the *Ecole Maternelle* (nursery). *Cycle 2* the *Grande section de Maternelle* and the first two years of the *Ecole Elémentaire* (Key Stage 1). *Cycle 3* is the top section of the *Ecole Elémentaire*, CM1 and CM2 (Key Stage 2). The table below sets out the equivalent year groups.

Ecole primaire			
Ecole maternelle	*toute petite section*	2 year-olds	
Cycle 1	*petite section*	3 and 4 year-olds	early years
	moyenne section	4 and 5 year-olds	KS1 reception
Cycle 2	*grande section*	5 and 6 year-olds	KS1 Year 1
Ecole élémentaire	*cours préparatoire (CP)*	6 and 7 year-olds	KS1 Year 2
	Cours elémentaire 1 niveau CE1 (level 1)	7 and 8 year-olds	KS2 Year 3
Cycle 3	*Cours elémentaire 2 niveau CE2* (level 2)	8 and 9 year-olds	KS2 Year 4
	Cours moyen (CM1)	9 and 10 year-olds	KS2 Year 5
	Cours moyen (CM2)	10 and 11 year-olds	KS2 Year 6

IUFM trainees need to teach in all three *cycles* in the course of their training. If they are coming to England towards the end of their course, they will almost certainly require a specific age group with whom to work, as they will have completed a placement in two *cycles* already and the third will therefore be specified. Some may also have an extended piece of work on a topic of their choice, a *mémoire professionnel*, to write while they are with you.

- **Establish efficient channels of communication with the trainee and higher education institution.**
- **Be as clear as possible about assessment requirements from the outset.**
- **Ensure that this information is passed on to participating class teachers** (see Chapter 4).

SELECTING HOST PRIMARY SCHOOLS

ADVICE FOR HIGHER EDUCATION INSTITUTIONS

As the ITT Primary Languages Project and other linked schemes involving teacher trainees from abroad expands, so does the need to find primary schools to host the native speakers. There are several ways to do this.

The most straightforward way may be to start by inviting primary schools already in partnership with the higher education institution to consider taking native speaker trainees. A key feature of the ITT project is that each UK trainee is partnered with a 'buddy' trainee from the partner institution abroad. The simplest solution is to find a primary school hosting an English trainee who is participating in the ITT project and will therefore be abroad for four weeks. In this case, the native speaker trainee simply goes into their English partner's school, which has a four-week period when the English trainee is away. The primary school then mentors the native speaker trainee in place of the English trainee.

Where a primary school is large enough to be able to accept two or three English primary languages trainees into different classes, they may be willing to accept the same number of native speaker trainees at the point they come for their school placement in England. This arrangement has the advantage that it may not always be necessary to pay the primary schools additionally for taking the native speaker trainees, as the latter are effectively replacing the English trainees who are abroad for one of their teaching placements. From the school's point of view, this means that they are not undertaking additional work but rather working instead with a different trainee, who happens to be a native speaker and can therefore offer their school an extra three or four weeks of native speaker input to boost their primary languages programme at some point in the school year. On the other hand, it may be appropriate according to local circumstances, to negotiate additional payment.

Anne Dareys

Anita Rowell

Where there are an insufficient number of partnership primary schools, Anne Dareys from St Martin's College, Lancaster, tells us that preliminary selection through informal networking can be a useful starting point. This is followed up more formally through a mail shot. She points out that, 'It does not always matter if schools already teach primary languages or not, what really counts is their **willingness to be involved in the ITT project**'.

In order to comply with the National Languages Strategy recommendations that the 'KS2 language-learning programme must ... be delivered at least in part in class time (DfES 2002: 16), it will be necessary to seek schools which are willing to timetable the primary languages work as part of the curriculum and do not rely solely on after school or lunchtime clubs, although these are useful additional means of using a native speaker's input. Christine Allan of Leeds Metropolitan University adds, 'Our first choice is **enthusiastic partnership schools**, which are also, in varying degrees, introducing a primary language'.

Anita Rowell of Bradford College advises choosing primary schools where there is a genuine interest in primary languages and where the languages are timetabled. If there is additional support available from a visiting specialist teacher from a linked secondary school this can also be a bonus. If the assistant is based in the secondary school as well, there will be plenty of opportunities for them to share teaching ideas and plan to team teach with the visiting secondary teacher (see Chapter 7, Jo Biddle and Laurent).

From the pupils' point of view, of course, it may be that there is little to be gained from having input from a native speaker teacher trainee when this cannot be sustained over the longer term.

It will therefore be vital to find ways of building on the experience of having the 'boost' to the language programme provided by the native speaker.

 Try to use schools in close proximity to the campus or their accommodation for ease of transport for the native speakers.

Alison Taylor, from the University of the West of England suggests using host families and inviting placement primary schools who are receiving the trainees to consider offering accommodation to the visiting trainee(s). This can solve transport problems, as the trainee will accompany their host teacher into school each morning. The host teacher does not need to be the teacher in whose class the native speaker trainee is teaching. Alternatively, parents of pupils or other families in the school locality may be used.

As we have seen above, native speaker assistants may be shared between several primary schools or be placed in a single school, according to local requirements. The table below sets out some of the advantages and disadvantages from the assistants' point of view of working in a number of primary schools.

Multiple placements	
Positive aspects	**Negative aspects**
• Instructive • Stimulating • Offers variety	• Less opportunity to get know one school really well • Harder to recall pupils' names and get to know them • Change of faces, teaching accommodation, administrative arrangements can take a while to get used to

Primary schools

With the exception of native speakers who are regular members of a primary school staff and trainees on full-time placements, try to avoid timetabling Foreign Language Assistants or Comenius Assistants on either a Friday or Monday. This will ensure that they have one full non-contact day per week, on which they can visit places of interest or follow courses to improve their English.

Secondary schools

If your native speaker is going to work in more than one primary school, try to use two schools which are close together. If you work in a family or cluster of primary schools, perhaps you can organise the days in the participating primary schools in such a way that transport problems are avoided, although this may be more difficult in rural locations with spread out primary schools.

• • • • •

Until languages become more established throughout KS2 in primary schools, it may be hard for a single primary school to find sufficient hours to employ a native speaker assistant solely in the one school. In this case, sharing an assistant with another primary school, or receiving one who also teaches in a cluster secondary school, can be a positive solution. Generally, however, we would suggest that native speaker assistants are employed in a maximum of three schools, in order to ensure that they can integrate into the host primary school community.

The next chapter suggests ways in which hosts can make sure that the native speaker really gets to know people and that their visit to the primary school is enjoyed by everyone.

4. Preparing the host primary schools

GUIDELINES FOR LEAs, HIGHER EDUCATION INSTITUTIONS AND SECONDARY SCHOOLS

Whether you are an LEA, a higher education institution or a secondary school organising native speaker placements in your associated primary schools, it will be essential to prepare primary schools for their role in hosting a native speaker. This chapter offers some suggestions for the kinds of topics you may wish to include in briefing meetings for primary colleagues. Advice aimed directly at primary schools can be found in Chapter 5, which focuses on preparing for the native speakers particularly from a primary school's point of view.

BRIEFING MEETINGS

Briefing meetings relating to native speaker assistants may be incorporated into larger mentor meetings when, for example, a higher education institution may invite teachers from all its partnership primary schools to attend a half- or whole-day session, dedicated to giving information about forthcoming teaching placements. A specific slot could be allocated to teachers involved in hosting primary languages trainees from home and abroad, geared to their specific needs.

If this is not possible, it will still be essential to invite teachers to find out about what hosting a native speaker assistant or teacher trainee is going to entail. It is helpful to invite not only the nominated class teachers who are likely to receive the native speakers, but also **headteachers** and the **primary languages co-ordinators**. This is because the support of senior management is crucial in helping ensure that the native speaker's time in primary school is successful, both from their own point of view and from the host school's. At Southampton University, an information sheet about the primary languages ITT project is provided. This summarises key issues about the contractual agreements between the Teacher Training Agency and the host and partner institutions as it relates to the school-based training for native speakers. Extracts from the briefing paper ('The school-based exchange placement') prepared for primary teachers receiving French trainees in 2002/03 can be seen overleaf.

The School of Education at the University of Durham and St Bede's School, Lanchester help participating primary schools prepare for their role as hosts to foreign trainees. In the first year their documentation included the following guidance:

- You will receive a brief description of your trainee, including areas of interest, as well as an estimate of linguistic competence based on the Common European Framework.
- The French trainees have police clearance.
- They are in their second year of training, having passed a competitive examination at the end of their first year.
- If students are coming as a group, suggest they share resources which they can use in rotation around schools.
- After an initial period of observation, the trainee can be used in a supportive role similar to a classroom assistant.

- As the trainee becomes acclimatised, he or she can be asked to teach whole classes; teaching French to whole classes will instil confidence.
- Subsequently, subjects such as mathematics and practical subjects lend themselves to teaching in English even by the less confident trainee.
- The subject mentor should use professional judgement in guiding the trainee as to which areas to teach in English, according to linguistic competence.

Self-assessment of English language competence can be helpful and the native speakers can be invited to describe themselves in a little 'pen portrait' which helps teachers both to plan ways of incorporating their interests and to build on their strengths, where possible. For example:

*Je vis dans un petit village à la montagne. J'aime skier, faire des randonnées. Je joue également au badminton. J'aime beaucoup la musique: je joue du synthétiseur.**

*J'ai déjà enseigné un an, dans une classe de maternelle. Je pratique la boxe.***

*   I live in a little village in the mountains. I like skiing and hillwalking. I also play badminton and really like music and play keyboard.

**   I've already taught for a year, in a nursery class. I like boxing.

The school-based exchange placement

Supporting the statutory curriculum

Each of the trainees from France is training to become a primary generalist with a specialism in English and their English should be good. They will be keen to get involved in supporting teaching in your class in whatever way you think fit. They have been told that they cannot teach unless they plan beforehand.

The trainees have already successfully completed two teaching placements in schools in France. They are now undertaking their **third** school-based placement, this time **entirely in England**. The placement in France, which their counterparts are doing, is a so-called *stage en responsabilité*, which means that the French trainees take **full responsibility for all teaching during the placement**. Clearly, that is not possible here, given the constraints of the national curriculum, and the need for the trainees to get to know the English school system and familiarise themselves with your schemes of work, ways of teaching and the children in your class. However, they **will expect to teach as much as possible**, and the school-based training should incorporate a variety of teaching opportunities from small groups to whole-class work, some of it alongside you in a team teaching mode, and other sessions 'solo', where appropriate.

Supporting primary French

Even if your school does not yet teach any French, or your trainee is working in Key Stage 1, the trainees from Alsace have come prepared to set up a **display** of authentic materials and pictures etc to use as a basis for discussion with the children about aspects of life in France or French-speaking parts of the world. They will also expect to teach some French, even if it is simple language, finger and action rhymes and songs. If your school has a more established programme in French, they will support its delivery.

Extract from briefing for primary schools receiving teacher trainees

Certainly any information received about the native speaker's interests and prior experience can be usefully shared.

At higher education institution/school partnership meetings Anne Dareys advises going through roles and responsibilities. It will be necessary to make clear whether or not primary colleagues are required to observe the native speaker teaching and to what extent they should provide oral and written feedback on the lessons. Primary teachers also need to know how many observations are required per week and the format these should take. For example, they may be required to use the same lesson feedback forms, which are used for the rest of the primary curriculum, in which case they will be familiar with them already. On the other hand, the higher education institution abroad may have requested that their own forms are used, in which case these may have been translated into English for use on the school placement here. The overall headings are likely to be similar but the layout may be different.

! tip **These preliminary briefing meetings are a means of getting everyone 'on board'. If you do not meet with all colleagues, misunderstandings can arise about the role of the host teachers and the native speakers.**

Christine Allan, from Leeds Metropolitan University, who works with undergraduate teacher trainees, emphasises that these meetings prior to the visit to discuss arrangements and the programme are 'essential'.

In addition, there may be weekly review forms and a summative report required at the end of the teaching placement. Again, primary schools need to be quite clear as to the form this reporting is going to take. In Southampton and Hull Universities, for example, a specific form has been created for use as the final report on the native speaker's placement. There may also be a deadline for the completion of this form. The summative form used by Hull and its partner institution in Nancy Metz can be seen overleaf.

If the native speakers are participating in an induction programme put on by the LEA or the higher education institution, this also needs to be flagged up and the nature of the content shared to avoid primary school colleagues repeating information.

Native speaker assistants who are Foreign Language or Comenius Assistants, or from the local community will also need ongoing support (see Chapter 5) and primary schools receiving a Comenius Assistant will be required to attend a briefing meeting held by the British Council Education and Training Group.

I U F M

Institute for Learning

l o r r a i n e

Relations Internationales

Joint Training Initiative
Report from English Host School

Trainee : ....

School : ....

THE UNIVERSITY OF HULL

Centre for Educational Studies

Please read the notes overleaf and then assess your trainee under the categories below

Professional values: Attitude, effort, relationships with colleagues & pupils, contribution to the general life of the school	
Subject knowledge: Competence in English when communicating with pupils & staff	
Subject knowledge: Trainee's progress in English over the teaching practice	
Teaching: Preparation of lessons	
Teaching: (of French) Teaching ability; pupil & classroom management	
Teaching: (of other subjects in English) Teaching ability; pupil & classroom management	
Teaching: Trainee's self-assessment of effectiveness of pupils' learning	

(Further comments may be added on the reverse of this form.)

Signature : .... Name : ....

Date : .... Position : ....

PRACTICAL ORGANISATION

Apart from the administrative matters highlighted above, it will also be helpful to discuss with primary colleagues other practical organisational issues to help them plan for the native speaker. Fred Lacey, from South Gloucestershire, advises schools to plan carefully to maximise the experience of having a native speaker.

A useful checklist of items for discussion by a primary school staff is as follows:

- with which National Curriculum year groups/classes is the native speaker going to work?
- within foreign language lessons?
- in other curriculum areas? (essential for Comenius Assistants and teacher trainees)
- in projects, special days, on visits?
- where is the native speaker going to teach?
- who is going to be responsible for the native speaker?

Foreign Language Assistants, Comenius Assistants and native speakers from the local community may be involved with primary languages teaching across a number of classes and year groups in their host primary school(s). In contrast, teacher trainees from abroad are likely to be attached to one class only, which they will teach in a similar way to a student teacher from this country on school-based placement.

Primary schools will also need to think carefully not only about the way in which they are going to use the native speaker but where they are going to teach, as there are several possibilities.

WHERE IS THE NATIVE SPEAKER GOING TO TEACH?

Think in advance about where the native speaker is going to work. Both in-class and working with small groups are typically ways of using native speakers and it is essential to plan whether the native speaker will take children out, or work with the teacher in the main classroom.

If their language work is incorporated into an ongoing workwheel of tasks, the language becomes part and parcel of normal class work, gives the teacher a chance both to monitor and to participate, learning alongside the children. Mutual support can be offered and it is also not so frantic!

Indeed, not only is the native speaker assistant's work in the classroom alongside the teacher important of itself, it also helps integrate the assistant as a member of staff with proper status in the eyes of the children and other teachers in the school.

The relationship between teacher and native speaker assistant needs to be viewed as a partnership and lessons planned to exploit the different strengths which each possesses. On the one hand, the class teacher knows his or her pupils intimately and has built up a special relationship with them, on the other, the native speaker has the target language at their finger tips.

Richard Smith of Trafalgar Junior School in Richmond upon Thames describes the way a Foreign Language Assistant, Delphine, has recently worked in his school. He tells us, Delphine worked alongside the class teacher, with the whole class and **with the class teacher involved**. This also offered an **element of INSET**.

Delphine

Advantages of having the native speaker working **alongside** the primary class teacher are summed up below.

Advantages for class teachers	Advantages for children	Advantages for native speaker
Teacher can see how individual pupils are responding	All children have similar exposure to the native speaker	The teacher is there to model effective practice/language to use when managing a classroom
Presence of the native speaker can help the teacher's subject knowledge: pronunciation, slang, cultural dimension	Children can see that the teacher values the native speaker's sessions. The foreign language is given higher status	The teacher can support the native speaker with class control if necessary
Teachers feel part of the foreign language experience	Seeing their teacher participate can encourage children to join in too	Some activities, such as teaching a song, are more suited to whole-class presentation, rather than small groups
Teachers can try out ideas introduced by the native speaker later in the week	The native speaker input is revisited by both teachers and pupils who gain additional practice and confidence	The native speaker has a chance to gain understanding of appropriate teaching and learning styles in the primary classroom

You may find that some native speakers prefer to withdraw small groups because they can develop their teaching skills under less pressure and feel more confident working on their own, whereas they are more on edge when teaching in front of an experienced class teacher.

The **disadvantage** of withdrawing groups to a location outside the classroom is that the teacher can neither monitor nor support the native speaker and is less likely to be involved in the language work and therefore less able to carry it on in-between sessions.

The following comment from a native speaker assistant indicates some of the pros and cons of an assistant working too far away from the main teaching area. The native speaker says:

I thoroughly enjoyed working with pupils independently. It made closer contact with the pupils possible and the atmosphere was friendly, but unfortunately I did not know what was happening in the classroom, what the children were learning and what their level was exactly.

The table below sets out some of the advantages and disadvantages of extracting children to work with the native speaker.

Withdrawal in small groups	Pros	Cons
Withdrawal to a quiet area outside the main classroom	Good for listening/speaking tasks where children need to be able to hear in order to discriminate foreign language sounds or be understood.	Libraries are not suitable for songs or activities involving movement because of rise in noise level.
Withdrawal to a communal open area	The space might be suitable for games (but this will depend on whether other open-plan teaching spaces are within earshot). More intensive practice possible.	If other pupils and staff are passing through or speaking English nearby this may make it difficult for children to concentrate. Less frequent meetings with the native speaker, as children wait their turn with the assistant to come round.

The following quote from a primary teacher in Kew shows how, even though the Foreign Language Assistant worked with small groups separately from the class teacher, nonetheless her work was carefully planned and supervised and because this was so, the children benefited from the small group work.

> *Isabelle took out groups of nine from the class, while the class teacher took the rest of the class for French. She followed the work planned by the class teacher, enabling the children to receive more focussed attention.*

One primary teacher who **works together with the native speaker** in the primary classroom says that she sees her role as supporting and encouraging the children and managing behaviour, if required. Another teacher adds:

> *I prefer to be present all the time, joining in where appropriate and practising the key words and phrases. This enables me to do more practice at registration and other moments during the week.*

Sometimes it can be tempting to use the time the native speaker is working with the class to catch up on other pressing tasks but as Doris' remark indicates, doing so can be quite demoralising for the native speaker. As Doris from Quebec put it:

I did not like it when the teachers were doing something else in the class during my lessons, like marking or working on the computer ...

Doris

 If you do decide that it is best for the native speaker to work with small groups of children:
- **try to ensure that the location is within earshot;**
- **provide a list of children's names;**
- **check whether specific equipment is required (a cassette recorder, CD player or occasional access to a video, paper and pencils).**

Of course, you can start the native speaker's session with a whole-class slot of around fifteen or twenty minutes and follow this up with small group work. If the native speaker has already worked alongside the teacher in the classroom, this should also help them integrate the teaching in any small group sessions more closely with the work of the class as a whole. By planning and collaborating with the class teacher, the native speaker should have a better grasp of the various teaching and learning styles within the class and their small group sessions should be enhanced both in methodology and content.

 If the native speaker is working with the whole class, do give them a seating plan and a class list.

If you prefer to avoid the upheaval of children going in and out of the classroom in order to work with the native speaker in small groups, an alternative arrangement (space permitting) is to split the class and for the native speaker to teach half the children, while you teach the remainder. This compromise makes class management easier for the native speaker and not withdrawing successive small groups permits activities requiring longer slots of time. The downside, however, is that you will not be able to participate and **this really is a missed opportunity.** Jo Cole enthuses:

The Foreign Language Assistant is often keen to develop role-play activities which is marvellous for the children and gives the non-specialist primary class teachers a chance to learn, by observing how it can be done. They can have a go with their children during their own class time and the assistant will then support the continuation and development of a role-play situation in subsequent visits.

Where groups are going to be taught, make sure that each has an actual teaching slot of at least fifteen minutes and allow a few minutes 'movement time' between each group. About twenty minutes actual contact time is about right. In the words of one Foreign Language Assistant: 'It's all about time, about **enough time** to do things properly'.

GROUP SIZE

A maximum group size of eight and a minimum of four pupils is preferable, with six pupils about right. Allocation to groups also requires forethought, to avoid undesirable groupings. It is difficult for native speakers to cope if you sometimes send out very small groups and, on other occasions, large numbers of pupils, so that they never know who nor how many children to expect.

Plan the groups in advance. If you can organise your pupils into fixed rather than random groups, this gives the assistant greater opportunity to get to know the children and build relationships with them.

Provide a class or group list and ask the children to wear sticky name labels or badges if the assistant is working with several classes or in more than one school.

In one south west London LEA, early experience of allocating Foreign Language Assistants to primary schools indicated the desirability of providing some guidelines, in order to make the assistant feel comfortable. Sometimes, even small issues such as being asked to work in the corridor or in the library where other pupils are working, can be a surprise to the native speaker assistant and make them feel that their work is marginalized. A 'contract' such as this one, can therefore be helpful:

Foreign Language Assistant Scheme

This is to confirm that Stéphanie Santos will be working in your school on Tuesday mornings from 13 January to 9 March 2004.

In order for the Assistant to feel welcome and for the scheme to work efficiently, it would be appreciated if wherever possible:

- a quiet room with table and chairs is made available;
- pupils are organised into fixed groups each time;
- a list of pupils' names is provided;
- the minimum time allocated to each group is 20 minutes;
- a cassette or CD player, paper and pencils are made available;
- the teacher allows a few minutes at the end of each session to plan for next time.

If primary schools are sharing native speakers between several schools, the participating schools must agree on messages about dress code, working patterns, relationships with pupils and responsibilities such as record keeping.

Raising cultural awareness

It can be very worthwhile discussing with primary colleagues intercultural expectations and behaviour which may be typical of the native speakers (see Chapter 5). Raising awareness in advance can help prevent misunderstandings. For example, teachers will find that trainees from some European countries will be used to a very early start to school in the morning, a long, two-hour lunch break, when teachers often leave the school premises and go home to eat, and a late end to the school day, between 16.00 and 17.00. Other trainees from countries such as Germany may be accustomed to early starts at around 08.00, but also work continental 'half days' with formal lessons finishing at 13.00. French primary trainees who are in their second year of training, having passed the highly competitive *concours* at the end of their first year, will already have taught and if their placement in England is in the spring or summer terms, are likely to have completed all their *stage en tutelle* placements in France, where they are more fully supported, and will be expecting a *stage en responsabilité* when they take sole responsibility for teaching. They may also not be expecting the class teacher to remain in the classroom and will be unused to the presence of other adult helpers, teaching assistants or parents. Others will be surprised to find that primary schools in England are open all week and not closed on a Wednesday, as in France. English primary teachers and mentors will find that the trainee teachers from abroad are very appreciative of the mentoring and support which they receive in their English host schools.

● ● ● ● ●

This chapter has offered suggestions for ways in which LEAs, HEIs and secondary schools might help primary schools prepare to host a native speaker assistant. Chapter 5 deals with practical arrangements for immediately before the native speaker's arrival in the primary school.

5. Preparing for the arrival of the native speaker assistant

GUIDELINES FOR HOST PRIMARY SCHOOLS

This chapter offers some further suggestions to ensure that working with a native speaker runs smoothly. It deals with the need to appoint a mentor, offers some ideas for ways of preparing the native assistant for his or her role in school and the importance of ensuring that expectations are mutually understood. It also includes checklists for both mentors and incoming assistants, so that nothing too important is forgotten.

Of course, it is really crucial that as many colleagues as possible support the idea of working with a native speaker assistant and are informed about the potential benefits and ways in which they can be used to enhance a languages programme and, indeed, enrich the life of the school. First of all, do let all colleagues know in advance that you are considering engaging a native speaker and **decide together** how your primary school wants to work with them.

APPOINTING A MENTOR

You will need to designate someone to take charge of the placement/mentor the native speaker.

If the native speaker is shared concurrently between two or more primary schools, or between a primary and its associated secondary, **one** school must be designated as the host school and accept prime responsibility for the native speaker. Where a secondary school is involved, the mentor might be the secondary teacher with responsibility for primary languages outreach.

Where an LEA is involved, an adviser may assume overall line management, but schools must still take responsibility for the native speaker assistants.

In addition, all native speakers need a clear point of contact with a **named individual** in each **primary** school in which they will be working. The National Languages Strategy (2002: 16) states that all primary schools should appoint a primary languages co-ordinator. Andrew Portas of Ringwood School reports:

> *In each feeder primary, someone has been made responsible for acting as the Foreign Language Assistant Co-ordinator, thus ensuring that the native speaker's needs are met and that an appropriate timetable is organised.*

If you do not yet have such a co-ordinator or mentor, consider the following possibilities:

- Is there someone keen to take the role on?
- Clarify what the role is to entail.
- Is there perhaps a younger colleague who might have more in common with a young native speaker?

Anne Dareys from St Martin's College, Lancaster, receives teacher trainees. Anne says, that in her experience, some trainees come over-prepared with planned lessons and resources which do not always quite fit the context in which they find themselves. This is because some primary schools have been teaching primary languages for years, while others have only just begun, so trainees meet a wide range of clientele and do not necessarily know how to adapt their lessons. This is where having a mentor who can provide advance information and give regular feedback can really help the native speaker.

PREPARING YOUR NATIVE SPEAKER

Richard Smith

Richard Smith of Trafalgar Junior School in Richmond upon Thames advises:

Try to think about ways of maximising the experience for the assistants too and not simply what the school needs to get out of the arrangements. Look out for their particular strengths and sound them out about any ideas or preferences they may have.

If you are receiving your native speaker through a secondary school or higher education institution and have not received information about your native speaker's interests, do ask if there are any details you can have. Opposite (*Fiche de renseignements*) is an example extract from a native-speaker form. (See also pen portraits in Chapter 4.)

Native speakers are likely to work more effectively if you can give them a sense of ownership of their timetables and negotiate aspects of their work:

- take note of the skills and interests on the native speaker's application form;
- draft a timetable: this should be flexible;
- send to the assistant for comment (if the native speaker is coming from abroad);
- be prepared to re-negotiate on arrival.

Fiche de renseignements	
Votre nom et prénom	•••••• ••••••
Nom de l'action/mobilité/formation	*Formation croisée à Southampton*
Votre motivation	*Découvrir le système éducatif anglais et ses différents partenaires.*
Vos attentes	*Rencontrer des enseignants anglais, confronter nos expériences pédagogiques et travailler avec des enfants anglophones.*
Vos compétences linguistiques	*Deug et Licence en Langue, Civilisation et Littérature Etrangère: Anglais.*
Expérience internationale	*Néant.*
Expérience pédagogique	*Une année sur le terrain en poste fractionné: CM2 et Petite Section de Maternelle.*
Etudes antérieures	*Deug et Licence en Langue, Civilisation et Littérature Etrangère: Anglais.*
Passe-temps/intérêts	*Photographie: prise de vue et développement, pratiques sportives (danse), lecture, cinéma, théâtre.*
Site et groupe à l'IUFM d'Alsace	*Site de Strasbourg, groupe B1.*
Stages/Cycles	*Stage tutelle: cycle 2* *R2: cycle 3* *R3: cycle 1* *R4?*
Sujet de votre mémoire professionnel	*Construire ses connaissances sur l'Europe (démarche technologique et géographie).*
Demande d'habilitation en anglais	*OUI.*
Dominante en anglais	*OUI (groupe . . .)*

Nigel Pearson from Liverpool says:

> *Sometimes there can be difficulties settling in. It is a good idea to inform them in detail as to the nature of work and expectations and to draw on help and advice from the agencies such as CILT, the National Centre for Languages and the embassies and cultural institutes.*

CLARIFYING EXPECTATIONS

Always bear in mind the quite significant adaptation many native speakers have to make to a different system of education, a different teaching context and different expectations of the roles and responsibilities of teachers and pupils.

In Germany, for example, each *Land* or federal region, has its own autonomous education system and this includes the way teachers are trained. French and German trainees, who will both be in their second stage/year of teacher training, already have the status of 'civil servants' rather than students in their home countries. Trainees from France, in particular, are unused to working beyond their allocated hours. They can be taken aback at first when they discover the extent to which many primary school teachers remain late at school, planning sessions jointly and working and preparing beyond the official school day. They can also be intrigued by primary teachers' pastoral role in England, as well as additional duties such as playground duty. It is important to make clear your expectations about attendance at staff meetings, or in-service events. Spanish trainees are likely to be used to specialising in one or two curriculum subjects only and may be surprised at the breadth of primary generalists' knowledge.

You might have to clarify expectations about dress code and what is acceptable in your school. Teachers in some other European countries can have, what to English minds, appears a casual attitude to jeans at work and some trainees may not bring a skirt, unless forewarned! Phil Farrar, from the University of Hull, who receives German trainees, notes:

> *In Baden Württemberg teachers wear whatever they like in the classroom – shorts if it's very warm, so trainees will have to be told that, in general, jeans, along with other more unusual, or bizarre forms of dress, rings in noses, multicoloured hair, etc are a no-no.*
>
> *However, since everyone knows that the trainees are only here for a short period, many schools will make some allowance for this, up to a point, so there is no easy answer to the question, 'What shall I wear to school?' The best response is to ask the head of each school, or better still, ask them all when a preparatory meeting is arranged … this can provoke some interesting discussion.*

Some native speakers may not be used to being observed and come from a culture in which the teacher's classroom is very much her or his private domain. They may be unused to the presence of other adults in the room, or even in the vicinity, and may not be accustomed to open-plan teaching areas and the freedom of movement which is typical of many English classrooms. Some teacher trainees may not expect the class teacher to remain in the room once they have arrived and may expect to take on whole-class responsibility almost at once and find a period of initial observation a surprise.

Below are examples of some of the similarities and differences two trainees from France noted when they worked in English primary schools.

OBSERVATION TASKS SCHOOL-BASED PLACEMENT
Finding out about primary schools in England

1. Find out about your placement school – look at the school prospectus and talk to teacher.

Note down **key points** below: How is the school organised? Who is responsible for what? What is the structure of the week and the school day? What is similar to and different from France?

Similarities
- The organisation of the classroom: tables, groups and a mat
- The class is organised in mixed abilities groups.

Differences
- The abilities expected from children of 5/6 years old.
- The assemblies during which all the pupils gather for prayers or songs.
- The absence of separating walls with the other classroom.
- The team teaching.
- School uniforms.
- The role of the headteacher.
- The purpose of display.
- Smoking and non-smoking rules.
- Religious education.

OBSERVATION TASKS SCHOOL-BASED PLACEMENT
Finding out about primary schools in England

1. Find out about your placement school – look at the school prospectus.

Note down **key points** below: What is **SIMILAR TO AND DIFFERENT FROM** France?

Different: pupils' lunchbox – pupils' lunchtime – starting & finishing hours – assembly – lunchtime & after school clubs – houses: captain, points. Pupils get changed in the classroom for PE sessions – no notebooks to write down what has been learned & what must be known (a cahier du jour) – no marking – a great deal of team/staff work: meetings – each teacher is responsible for one subject, hands out the weekly lesson plans to the other teacher – one team manager (conformism/some weekly plans)

OBSERVATION TASKS SCHOOL-BASED PLACEMENT
Finding out about primary schools in England

1. Find out about your placement school – look at the school prospectus.

Note down **key points** below: What is **SIMILAR TO AND DIFFERENT FROM** France?

Y5-Y6: from 8 to 10 years old – 29 pupils sitting around five tables in groups of 6 to 8 – whiteboard – pupils' notebooks provided by the school – prayer corner – lunchchest – drawers – hangers inside the classroom – water bottles provided.

The following mentor's checklist contains a tick list of things it is useful to remember to do, in order to facilitate the native speaker's placement in your school.

Mentor's checklist

- ☐ Send a welcome letter, signed by the headteacher
- ☐ Send details of the school's website address
- ☐ Send a school prospectus with photos of the school and pupils
- ☐ Supply details of your primary languages project with some indication of the extent of pupils' prior knowledge of the language
- ☐ Send your school's Early Language Learning policy
- ☐ Send one or two examples of pupils' work which will give the native speaker an idea of the level they have reached (written, audio, video?)
- ☐ Provide key contact details (mentor's name, telephone number and e-mail address)
- ☐ Telephone or send an e-mail
- ☐ Arrange arrival details (when, where and to whom they should report on arrival)
- ☐ Send address and details of the accommodation arranged for them *
- ☐ Send an information pack about the local area, with details of public transport, for example
- ☐ Provide an indication of the climate and what clothes to wear
- ☐ Arrange first meeting
- ☐ Suggest that they prepare a short introductory presentation on an aspect of their background, e.g. a stand-up book with photos

* Bear in mind the native speaker's limited income when looking for suitable accommodation on their behalf. There may be members of the school staff who would welcome the assistant as a paying guest.

 If your school has had a native speaker before, it is really useful for the outgoing assistant to write a letter or send an e-mail to the new assistant, telling them what the job entails and what life is like in the local community. If the next native speaker is the same nationality, this can be in the assistant's own language. Extracts of such letters are offered here as illustration.

The pupils really like having things that they can see and touch, such as photos and items from the assistant's country. This has been a wonderful voyage of discovery for me and has made me determined to become an English teacher.

Gaëlle, Brittany

Gaëlle

Cécile

I have spent an exceptional eight months here. You will work about 12 hours a week, teaching pupils aged between 5 and 11. I had three or four schools a term and spent one day a week in each. Some teachers prefer you to teach whole classes, others will give you groups of children of between 5 and 15, for 20 to 40 minutes. You will not only teach French but also the culture. Photos of your family, your house and postcards of your town will all be useful. The eight months pass quickly, even too quickly … To be an assistant is an unforgettable experience. The primary school children are adorable and they love their French lessons! They are a pleasure to teach.

Cécile, Toulouse

Even if your native speaker belongs to the local community, they will still need details of the pupils' prior language learning experiences and where possible a scheme of work and suggestions for activities and resources. And if they do not know your primary school well, then a school brochure and the school's website will also be appreciated.

WHAT SHOULD ASSISTANTS BRING?

If the native speakers are coming from abroad, thinking these things through in advance will enable you to give them guidance as to the most appropriate materials to bring from their own country, to suit the time they are in your school. Stress the kind of visuals which primary age children find appealing and which will be most effective in whole-class presentations. Tell them to keep receipts and consider whether you will be able to reimburse them for any materials they are likely to leave with the school.

Bear in mind, that some native speakers will not be used to the kind of interactive, creative display work so common in UK primary schools. Sending a photo of a classroom might help inspire him or her!

You may find the following checklist a useful tool for your assistant.

Assistants' pre-departure checklist • Cultural dimension

- ☐ (Large) colour photographs of native speaker's family, friends, pets, home, town or school. If photographs can be made in electronic form, it will be possible to copy them onto the computer and project them large-scale using a data projector
- ☐ Real-life artefacts such as children's exercise books, pencils, colouring books, school timetable or homework diary, birthday, and Christmas, Easter or 'first day at school' cards
- ☐ BIG pictures and posters, particularly of FOOD!
- ☐ Colourful advertising brochures and catalogues
- ☐ Slides, videos, DVDs of stories or songs, flags, stamps, **simple** maps, **children's** atlas
- ☐ Food packets and wrappers, phone cards, foreign coins, 'pretend' euros, menus, drinks and ice cream lists, sweets and small authentic items for 'rewards'
- ☐ Stickers and badges

Assistants' pre-departure checklist • Language teaching

- ☐ Finger, action rhymes, songs
- ☐ CDs, videos, DVDs, cassettes of stories and songs
- ☐ Big books (although these are less commonly available abroad), story books with simple, familiar story lines, opportunities for repetition, participation and acting out and bold illustrations
- ☐ Puppets and cuddly toys
- ☐ Masks and straightforward instructions for paper folding, art and craft, making things and recipes for cooking
- ☐ Catalogues, leaflets, booklets, posters, children's comics and magazines

> *Bring anything that might strike children as original and uncommon as compared to what they can find in their own country.*
> (Christine, France)

> *Just bring ordinary things like a brochure from a theme park, or an advertisement from a supermarket. I also brought some food – German cake – which the children loved when we were talking about food.*
> (Simone, Germany)

> *With the little ones, I used a 'surprises bag'. In it, I had such things as a Canadian flag, a dollar bill with the Queen's head on it and photographs of wild animals found in my country.*
> (Doris, Quebec)

• • • • •

This chapter has dealt with arrangements prior to the native speaker assistant's arrival in primary school. The following chapter considers ways of supporting them once they have arrived.

6. Supporting your native speaker assistant

If your native speaker is coming **directly from abroad**, there are several things you can do to make him or her feel welcomed and valued right from the start. LEA personnel or ITT providers may have undertaken some of these tasks if your native speaker is coming through a scheme linked to the LEA or higher education institution. However, where schools have applied directly to the British Council for a Foreign Language or Comenius Assistant, remember that Assistants do appreciate it if they can be:

- met at the airport or station;
- provided with a host family, even if temporarily;
- given a lift to the accommodation;
- provided with a welcome meal – maybe at a local pub with a small group of staff;
- provided, if self catering, with a 'basics bag' (tea, coffee, milk, sugar, *croissants*, butter, cereals, cake) so that breakfast is available on the first morning and he or she doesn't have to rely on going out to a shop before anything else;
- given a welcome pack with a town plan showing the school, supermarket, Post Office, bank, bus and train stations, GP and dentist, and emergency numbers.

INDUCTION

If your native speaker has come to you via the LEA, a central induction meeting may have been arranged. There may be a charge to the school for this. Many Foreign Language Assistants working in primary schools find themselves in induction programmes intended for the majority of assistants, who are going to be teaching in a secondary school. Where induction is aimed at secondary assistants, it is helpful either to supplement it with sessions which pay attention to the different requirements of primary schools, or to provide an alternative programme with the specific needs of primary native speakers in mind. In Richmond upon Thames, primary Foreign Language Assistants are given a morning's induction before joining a larger session with local secondary assistants. This provides them with a useful opportunity to meet and to exchange contact details. Induction sessions such as this usually cover practical details, such as opening a bank account, obtaining a NI number and completing Inland Revenue forms. The second day of the induction period is spent on a school visit, to get a general feel of an English primary school and day three concentrates on feedback from the visits and lesson preparation.

Comenius Assistants will be eligible to attend briefing meetings held at the British Council. German Foreign Language Assistants will be able to attend a training day at their nearest Goethe Institut and will be provided with a pack of materials explaining the way the English school system works. The French embassy provides a booklet of teaching ideas, a 'toolkit' for language assistants, the *Boîte à outils*, but this is secondary orientated. Spanish-speaking assistants can consult the website of the Consejería de Educación y Ciencia at **www.cec-spain.org.uk**.

AN LEA INDUCTION PACKAGE

Where an LEA is able to appoint centrally one or more foreign language assistants, it is really worthwhile organising an induction package, as time spent on this at the beginning will reap dividends later. This is particularly the case if the native speaker is coming to Europe alone and for the first time, as was the case when Doris came to work in Richmond upon Thames from Canada (see below).

Primary Foreign Language Assistant:
Doris Villeneuve

Induction programme

26 September	Arrival at Heathrow 06.50 (Air Canada 0864). Anne Farren to collect and take to host family.
28 September	Introductory meeting with Anne Farren at the teachers' centre and lunch.
2 October	General visit to a primary school.
3 October	Introductory visits with Anne Farren to at least some host schools.
5 October	Lesson preparation with Anne Farren.
9 October	Induction session with Foreign Language Assistants from the LEA's secondary schools.

Teaching programme begins.

INDUCTION BY HIGHER EDUCATION INSTITUTIONS

Higher education institutions will also find it helpful to provide some element of induction for the native speaker trainees they are welcoming. The form this takes will depend on the point in the academic year when the trainees arrive. A unique feature of the ITT Primary Languages Project is the buddying of each trainee from England with a native speaker trainee. Thus the majority of trainees from mainland Europe will have a partner in the English higher education institution. If the English student partners are in the university (i.e. not on one of their school-based placements), it is worthwhile exploring whether the native speakers can join existing student groups, accompanying their 'buddies' to whatever sessions are being held. This is a straightforward way of helping both the English and native speaker trainees get to know each other speedily and naturally. Opposite is an extract from an induction programme at Southampton University.

Programme for 22 February to 22 March 2003

Date	Activity	Notes
Saturday 22 February	French trainees arrive at Bournemouth airport. Flight FR 8096 15.45. Met by Cynthia. Transport to South Stoneham Halls of Residence, Wessex Lane, where accommodation in single rooms has been booked. 19.00 meal at Highfield Pub, Highfield Lane, Southampton.	Welcome pack of food provided for Sunday morning.
Sunday 23 February	Free morning and early p.m. 15.00 – 18.00 all students (Southampton and French) meet Room 2003, ground floor Building 34. University. Formal welcome by Head of School of Education. Briefing, social, cultural familiarisation. Buffet meal.	Southampton trainees present English school system to French trainees.
Monday 24 February	French trainees into university. Join English partners for Foundation sessions.	Half-term week: schools closed. Lunch with partners in University (students pay for themselves).
Tuesday 25 February	French trainees into university. Foundation sessions.	
Wednesday 26 February	French trainees in university. Core subjects.	Cynthia in CILT.
Thursday 27 February	French trainees in university. Core subjects.	
Friday 28 February	French trainees in university. ICT a.m. 11.00–12.30 French joint work on ICT-related tasks. Lunchtime – eat together (pay separately). 14.00–15.00 First Impressions: brief review meeting with French trainees to check how first week has gone. Information from English trainees about partnership schools/transport/classes, etc.	PGCE Co-ordinator briefs students about primary school placements in Hampshire.
Saturday 1 March	French group visits Winchester (Cathedral city, shops, etc). Cynthia and some English trainees accompany French group.	
Sunday 2 March	With English partners, free choice.	

A similar programme operates at St Martin's College, Lancaster. Drawing on previous experience, Anne Dareys advises:

Trainees wanted to feel part of the student community, not a separate group, so we now integrate them into the sessions in Maths, PE and Music which their English partner trainees are attending and the native speakers love it.

Certainly if the native speaker trainees can join with their English 'buddies' this helps orientate them and prepares them for their time in school. Alternatively, you may wish to arrange a special programme for the trainees from abroad. At Reading University, visiting native speakers have a series of especially arranged seminars, which they attend as a separate group. As can be seen from the programme extract below, topics include the school system in England, the National Curriculum, National Literacy and Numeracy Strategies and primary languages pedagogy, and are taught by a variety of tutors.

Timetable for university-based study week at Bulmershe Court			
Week 2	University-based study		
Monday 26 January	**Building 7 – conference room** 10.00–13.00 1. Overview of first week in schools. 2. The organisation of primary education in England. 3. Modern Foreign Languages in primary education in England: historical perspectives and current status		**Building 7 – conference room** 14.00–16.00 Modern Foreign Languages in primary education – pedagogy: strategies employed in the classroom appropriate to the chronological and cognitive development of the children
Tuesday 27 January	**Building 9 – *room to be advised*** 10.00–12.00 Science in the primary National Curriculum	**Building 7 – Conference room** 12.15–12.50 Packed lunch to meet director primary PGCE and other PGCE tutors if possible	**Building 9 – primary base** 13.00–13.50 A look at the resource centre for primary education **The National Centre for Language and Literacy** 14.00–15.30 To view primary publications
Wednesday 28 January	**Building 9 – room BG26** 10.00–12.00 The National Literacy Strategy		Free Private/IUFM study
Thursday 29 January	**Building 9 – room B120** 10.00–12.00 The National Numeracy Strategy		**Building 7 – room 108–109** 14.00–15.00 Ideologies of primary education in England
Friday 30 January	Free Private/IUFM study		

In addition to formal input on educational issues, native speakers will appreciate an opportunity to get know the local area. So for example, Anne Dareys organises a three-day orientation programme at St Martin's, Lancaster, before the visiting teacher trainees go into primary schools. This includes a tour of the campus, a visit to Lancaster, a welcome pack, registration so that trainees have e-mail (a must!) and a temporary library card.

In Southampton University, the welcome meeting has involved the English partner students each taking it in turn to present an aspect of English primary school life to their native-speaker buddies. Below is an example of a handout on literacy prepared by a trainee.

Literacy

◆ 'Literacy' means English.

◆ Generally, literacy is taught once per day, for one hour. This is called the 'Literacy hour' and has a formal structure.

◆ The structure and objectives are set out in the **National Literacy Strategy** (a governmental document).

◆ The **National Curriculum** sets out the requirements that have to be met by the end of the year.

◆ Structure:
15 min – Text work (story/article): **whole class**.
15 min – Sentence/word work (grammar/punctuation/spelling): **whole class**.
20 min – Independent activity: **whole class**. **Teacher works with small group**.
10 min – Plenary: **whole-class**.

Plenary = conclusion of summary lesson.

◆ The role of the teacher = to *teach*, not to wander around, looking for problems.

Planning

◆ In most schools the planning for literacy will be done every week. This is a **weekly plan**. It tells the teacher what should be covered by the end of the week.

◆ Trainee teachers are expected to use the weekly plan to write **individual lesson plans** (one detailed plan for *each* lesson.

◆ To find a copy of our blank plans go to **www.soton.ac.uk/~pgce**. Click on 'core subjects'. English, Maths and Science template plans can be printed.

MAKING YOUR NATIVE SPEAKER FEEL WELCOME IN SCHOOL

Particularly when the placement is short, it is vital that native speakers feel at home and establish themselves speedily in school. You can help to welcome them into the school community by:

- informing all members of staff about the native speaker's appointment;
- treating the native speaker as a regular member of staff;
- deciding on how to address them and whether children should use the native speakers' first or family names;
- introducing them to colleagues – photos help – including the school secretary and support staff;
- introducing them to the pupils (telling the children what the native speaker is there for);
- providing them with an ID badge if necessary.

Practical information might include:

- details of the school timetable;
- start and finish of each school day;
- times of playtimes and lunchtime.

THE MENTOR'S ROLE

It is at this point that the mentor's role will come into its own, as primary schools are extremely busy places and, in the pressure of day-to-day demands, it is easy for people to appear unwelcoming to a newcomer when, in fact, they are merely preoccupied with commitments.

A tour of the school, which can be undertaken by the mentor or by pupils, might include:

- location of toilets, tea/coffee making facilities, canteen and lunch arrangements;
- key noticeboards;
- where to pick up any mail or messages.

If you have not already sent it in advance, an induction pack with a copy of your school's early language learning policy will be something worthwhile for the native speaker to take home with them and browse through at the end of their first day.

Check whether the native speakers have had the opportunity to participate in an induction programme and whether they are familiar with the Key Stages, National Literacy and Numeracy Strategies, Excellence and Enjoyment and the Key Stage 2 Framework for MFL.

All categories of native speaker assistants will find it helpful if they can:

- participate in a typical primary school day (attend assemblies, hymn practice, be part of lunchtime activities);
- shadow a pupil;
- shadow the class teacher/visiting languages teacher with whom they are going to work.

Informal contact between the native speakers and the children and teachers with whom they will be working will provide opportunities for you to find out more about their background and interests and tailor their timetable and contribution accordingly.

OBSERVING PRIMARY TEACHERS AT WORK

It is advisable for native speakers to start with a period of guided observation, during which they can sit in on a variety of classes. If they can visit different year groups and observe across subject areas, they will begin to gain an overview of the primary curriculum. This is vital for native speakers who are teacher trainees.

Even those who are practising or intending to become teachers in their own country need a programme which enables them to watch skilled primary teachers talking to children, holding books, using visuals, asking and answering questions, running Circle Time and managing a primary classroom. As Jo Cole, a primary AST from the International Learning and Research Centre in South Gloucestershire, points out:

> *Our French trainee teachers from the IUFM benefit from experiencing how a primary child spends their day in school. It is very important to explain our multi-sensory, kinaesthetic approach.*

If the native speaker can be present in the primary classroom on several occasions, getting to know the children and helping and participating in activities, this will help prepare them for their teaching role. Sandra, a Foreign Language Assistant from La Réunion, tells us:

> *After my arrival in England, I watched the language teachers and learned different methods of teaching. This gave me the opportunity to understand better what I was expected to do, because before coming to England, I did not know what I was going to do and how to be a French assistant in primary school.*

tip **If you are not very confident about the native speakers observing you teach the foreign language, why not watch one of the ELL videos produced by CILT, *Making it happen*, *Making it work*, or *Making it better*? These can form an ideal basis upon which to discuss differences and similarities the native speakers spot between teaching strategies in their own country and the way primary schools work in England.**

Sometimes it is possible to arrange for native speaker assistants to observe languages teaching in other primary schools in a local cluster with a more established programme. Where there is an AST or an advisory teacher who can observe alongside the native speakers, general principles arising from what is seen can feed into useful discussions on primary methodology.

If your native speaker is a teacher trainee, check with your higher education institution tutors whether or not native speakers who are teacher trainees have a booklet of tasks which they need to complete while on their placement. The example opposite shows the types of questions to which they may be seeking answers.

Where the teacher trainees or Comenius Assistants are going to be delivering parts of the primary curriculum via the medium of English, a foreign language for them, the challenge and hazards of working in another language should not be underestimated. Although many have a high level of English, sometimes the native speaker's command of written or spoken English can be insufficient for certain classroom tasks and teachers need to be prepared for this.

In any case, it will be helpful for all native speaker assistants if they write down the language of the classroom, noting what you say to praise, encourage, organise and control pupils. This will help them not only to use appropriate English when managing the classroom, but also incorporate phrases with which the pupils are already familiar from their class teacher. They should also be able to transfer some of the English expressions to simple target language, for use when they are teaching their mother tongue. Opposite is an example of an observation task focused on the target language of the English-speaking primary classroom.

Let native speaker assistants know what rewards there are for good behaviour and the sanctions there are for misbehaviour.

 Primary schools' policies focus on encouraging good behaviour through positive behaviour management strategies, rather than 'punishing' bad behaviour. Make sure that your native speakers are very familiar with rules, rewards and sanctions, as they may be used to a completely different system.

Phil Farrar from Hull University comments that discussions with German trainees revealed that German teachers in general are somewhat reluctant to praise. They will give lots of praise and encouragement to very young children in Key Stage 1, but less and less as the pupils grow older.

TTA Primary French Pilot Project 2002/2003
Improving your target language of the classroom

What are the key expressions that experienced primary teachers in England use to manage their lessons?

Using the headings below, note down examples in English of what the teacher says to carry out regular routines within the classroom. He or she will be using some of these expressions, instructions, comments, throughout the day.

What does the teacher say to:

- get the children into the classroom?
- get their attention, get them quiet?
- greet the children?
- settle them for registration?
- take the register?
- organise dinner money?
- move them to and from assembly?
- change the weather, day, date chart, celebrate birthdays?
- introduce activities?
- organise children into groups?
- tell children to work on their own?
- distribute materials?
- collect materials?
- praise children?
- tell children off?
- set homework?
- collect homework?
- talk about children's work?
- send the children out to play
- tidy up?
- dismiss the children at the end of the day?

Is there special language for PE/Science/ICT/Art/Music?

PREPARING TO TEACH

How often the native speakers meet particular classes will depend on individual arrangements in schools. Foreign Language Assistants and Comenius Assistants will probably only be in school for a short time each week and they will work with the primary languages teacher(s) and their classes for perhaps half an hour each.

In contrast, teacher trainees from abroad, will be attached to a single class 'full-time' during their month's visit and will be in school throughout the week, much like a normal teacher. As their placement goes on, you can expect them to take over an increasing amount of teaching. The pattern may go something like this:

Week 1	Week 2	Week 3	Week 4
observation and small group support	observation, small groups and team teaching	team teaching/start whole-class sessions	whole-class management

The school programme below allows the French trainees to be in the university on a Wednesday, a day when they would typically not be in a school in France.

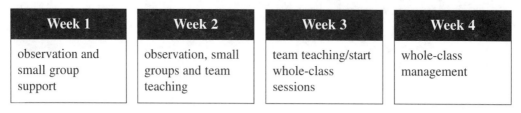

School programme				
Monday	**Tuesday**	**Wednesday**	**Thursday**	**Friday**
19/01/04 University based	Meet school staff and be inducted into school	University based	Observation and group work under direction of class teacher	Observation and group work under direction of class teacher
26/01/04 Work in school	Work in school	University based	Work in school	Work in school
02/02/04 Work in school	Work in school	University based	Work in school	University based

Below is an extract from a briefing for native speaker trainees participating in an exchange with the University of Southampton.

You will be expected to be in school from around 08.30 each day and to remain there until the end of the school day (around 15.00–15.30) Your headteacher and class teacher will be expecting you.

You will start by doing some **observation** in your partner's classroom and later, by arrangement, you will observe **other classes**, age groups and activities in the primary school to which you are assigned. You will also do the **observation activities** in this handbook.

It will be be particularly helpful for you to watch the **Literacy and Numeracy** hours and the teaching of English. You will also find other subject areas, the foundation subjects, across the curriculum valuable and interesting. Also try to participate in an English school assembly.

It is suggested that you first work with **small groups and then support the class teacher in whatever way is most helpful for them and suitable for you**, according to your confidence and competence in English.

You may have the opportunity to help with some teaching of French to young beginners. At the time of writing, in most schools in our locality the children you will see will only just be beginning French lessons. Some will be learning within the curriculum but others will be attending a lunchtime or after-school club on a voluntary basis. So you will need to keep it short, simple and lively.

As you become familiar with the English primary curriculum you will be able, in agreement with the class teacher, to teach whole classes in a subject in which you feel comfortable. This might be Art, Music, the Maths starter, small group in Literacy, Citizenship, games in the hall or playground (with the class teacher present), Geography, History or ICT. At the end of the placement the class teacher will complete a **brief written report** on your teaching and contribution.

PLANNING

The respective roles of the primary class teacher and the native speaker assistant need to be considered. Who is leading and who is supporting? Also consider opportunities for the native speaker to get involved, for example:

- Is the native speaker in school at a time of year when particular festivals are taking place, for example, harvest, Christmas, Epiphany, Easter, Mother's Day, or festivals from his or her own country and culture?
- Which language and cultural topics is the native speaker going to present?
- Could he or she help with setting up a link with a school abroad, perhaps by telephoning to link schools or assist children sending e-mail messages?
- Could the native speaker help run children's clubs or accompany trips?
- Could he or she produce displays about his/her home country, which could be open to parents and other members of the community, to raise awareness of the international dimension more widely?

<u>VENDREDI .13. JUIN</u>

matinée sportive (corde à sauter) pour supporter les malades du cœur.

<u>LUNDI 16 JUIN</u>

MATIN 2 groupes de 4 (Wanda's class)
→ nombres
→ monnaie
⮡ feuille /exercices.

AM "festival" des arts à l'école (year 3 & 4)
→ chaque enfant présente ses performances artistiques (danse, musique, théâtre...) au reste de l'école.

<u>MARDI 17 JUIN</u>

MATIN • french speakers
→ dictée de nombres
→ exercice sur l'heure refait et corrigé

AM " festival des arts " (year 5 & 6)

An example of a trainee French teacher's programme

Right at the beginning of their placement, before they start to work in the classroom, native speakers need time to plan and prepare. It is easier for them to do so effectively, if a scheme of work is available which can act as a framework for their teaching. The Non-statutory Schemes of Work for Key Stage 2 are a helpful starting point (QCA 2000) as well as the Key Stage 2 Framework (2005). You will find many useful examples of schemes of work and lesson plans in the on-line *NACELL best practice guide* (see **www.nacell.org.uk/bestpractice/index.htm**).

Andrew Portas from Hampshire describes how he supports assistants:

> *The Primary Languages Project has been set up so that primary staff observe MFL specialists deliver the scheme of work throughout an academic year before they then teach the scheme of work themselves. They are supported by detailed lesson plans, resources and half-termly INSET by the MFL Advanced Skills Teacher responsible for primary languages. The Foreign Language Assistant has access to these lesson plans, materials and training, and observes MFL teaching as well.*

In the above case, the Foreign Language Assistant starts teaching after two weeks' observation, as he or she is going to be available to primary schools for several months and the lead-in time to teaching can be generous. In other situations, the observation period may have to be shorter but should still take place. The following support is likely to be helpful:

- Where native speakers have been employed in previous years, it is helpful if new assistants can refer to written records describing what their predecessors have done with which groups (see Chapter 8).
- Where a school welcomes a native speaker for the first time, notes of vocabulary, structures and activities which have already been introduced will help them to orientate their presentations. Similarly, native speakers should be required to keep notes of their own contributions, which the usual primary languages teacher can build on or incorporate into her or his own planning once the assistant has gone.
- Provide a lesson plan template and talk through with the assistant how to plan a short session and reflect on it afterwards.
- Allow time for native speakers to familiarise themselves with resources.
- Show them how to access the NACELL (National Advisory Centre on Early Language Learning) website. This will be helpful in showing examples of shared practice in the *NACELL best practice guide* and the 'see a school' facility (**www.nacell.org.uk**).

On the subject of time for native speakers to access the Internet, St Bede's Specialist Language College reports that they give native speakers weekly twilight access to multimedia facilities and that students are very keen to use the Internet!

CREATING AND STORING JOINT RESOURCES

If there are several native speakers in your locality, it may be possible for them to meet in order to put together materials as a team, even across languages. Try to give them access to a variety of high quality materials from which to draw inspiration. French native speakers are always amazed at the wonderful displays, colour and interest in English primary classrooms. To facilitate this, make sure native speakers know about:

- teachers' or Comenius centres and ELL Regional Support Groups, which are likely to have a stock of published teaching materials, including photocopiable worksheets which can be referred to when planning and making resources;

- foreign cultural institutes and embassies which can provide a rich source of information and cultural resources, including posters;
- the CILT Resources Library which can be visited personally (transport/distance permitting);
- the NACELL website which incorporates a searchable database of primary languages resources.

Allocate a cupboard or shelf specifically for your native speaker, which houses in one central location lists of language activities undertaken, plus the associated resources. This will help them know exactly where to look for particular materials. Successive native speakers can add to these resources and, as newcomers, they will have the advantage of a cupboard of materials where they can see at a glance what their predecessors have used. Under one successful scheme, assistants compile a *booklet of teaching ideas*, which are added to each year and given to incoming native speakers as part of their induction.

Some native speaker trainees who intend to teach in their own country are keen to reuse the resources they have devised during their UK primary school placement in their future teaching and may even return home with them! Do make it clear that you would like the assistants to leave behind as many of the materials they have made as possible when they return to their country of origin. Resources developed could always be duplicated, ensuring one example is left behind for the next assistant and to support the class teacher to continue the primary languages work.

ONGOING IN-SCHOOL SUPPORT

Monitoring and support should enable you to nip in the bud any emerging difficulties so that they do not become an issue. Sometimes this will simply be liaising between your native speaker and the rest of your colleagues in whose classes they work, or with the secondary school, if appropriate. One mentor reports, 'Sometimes native speaker assistants need someone to act as a kind of confidant – at least until they have settled in and begun to adapt'. You will find that the more thorough the input at the start the easier it will be to resolve any problems later.

MONITORING AND REVIEWING PROGRESS

Once the assistants' teaching programme is underway, all categories of native speaker assistant, including those from within the local community, still need to be offered support, as it is not necessarily the case that they are trained teachers. Regular meetings to discuss difficulties and exchange ideas are helpful, as are monitoring visits where they are given feedback on their teaching. Where the LEA is providing assistants free of charge to primary schools, there is the issue of who is responsible for helping them with their work. It is useful to establish at the outset the extent to which help with, for example, behaviour management and differentiation, is the school's responsibility.

Probably the most difficult thing to achieve in the midst of the demands of a hectic primary school day is time to meet with the native speaker. Do, however, set aside a brief timetabled weekly slot to exchange information about what has been done in the primary languages sessions, for debriefing purposes and to plan future activities. Again, this is not so onerous, if one person is the mentor and has time set aside for this purpose.

 You may need to stress the importance of the weekly mentor sessions with your native speaker, as some may be participating in training programmes in their home countries, in which teachers rarely meet to plan and discuss together in the way which is typical of many UK primary school teams.

As Séverine, a Foreign Language Assistant from France points out:

 Don't be afraid to tell the assistant when something goes wrong. Feedback is essential and helps make progress.

If your native speaker is a teacher trainee, you will probably be completing written observations as soon as they start teaching, and conducting a weekly review to set targets for the following week. The ITT provider will also be meeting with the trainees early on in their month's placement, probably after the first two or three days, to check how things are going in the host school. You will need to be clear with your higher education institution as to the status of the trainee's placement – is assessment formative or summative? This will depend on the point in the academic year at which the trainee from abroad arrives – early on, and the placement is likely to be formative, but from mid-Spring onwards, the placement is almost certain to 'count' towards their final assessment in their home institution, with specific teaching standards to be met.

Teachers are likely to be having informal discussions and conversations with the native speaker assistants as they occur naturally. However, a mentor meeting can provide opportunities for reflection on teaching and help the assistants develop a variety of teaching and learning strategies.

TOPICS FOR MENTOR TIME

However naturally inspired at teaching, all native speaker assistants require methodological support, either as regards teaching their own language, or to help them use English to manage the classroom or to teach parts of the primary curriculum. Below are some suggestions for topics for mentor time.

- **Body language**: The importance of ensuring that children can see the assistant's mouth, face and body to help them listen attentively.

- **Presenting and practising new language**: Those teaching their own language may need support in how to present new language (vocabulary and structures) using varied and motivating repetition techniques and visual prompts. This is best undertaken in a team-teaching context, which will enable the helper to observe a specialist demonstrating a range of methodological approaches, e.g. chanting, repetition, language games and songs.

- **Developing a sequence of graded questions and answers**: All are likely to require support in developing a series of graded questions and answers, to ensure that all children can participate. It is helpful if they learn to move from closed questions (*ja/nein*) to open questions (*Wie viele Geschwister hast du?*).

- **Giving simple instructions**: Another area in which support needs to be given is target language use, especially ways of giving simple instructions for activities, combined with modelling and gestures.

- **Planning for target language use**: Many native speakers are unused to breaking down their own language into small attainable steps and may 'overwhelm' young learners by failing to simplify, or speaking too rapidly.

- **Involving children actively**: Some native speakers may come from teaching contexts in their home country in which there is little group work and may expect instead to teach whole classes in a rather formal way.

While it may seem obvious, it is important to stress eye contact and clarity, and ensuring all children are involved. Equally, assistants need to be encouraged to praise and to correct by modelling, that is saying the correct answer for the children to repeat.

It is useful if assistants have ample opportunity to observe and have access to resources and documentation to support learning, such as the QCA guidelines, CILT *Young Pathfinder* publications and commercial teaching resources. The CILT Early Language Learning videos, *Making it happen*, *Making it work* and *Making it better* also offer valuable examples of primary teaching.

 Some native speakers may be unfamiliar with the concept of *differentiation* and be unused to planning for children of different abilities and learning styles.

It will be helpful if, during the mentor time, the mentor and native speaker assistant are able to write a brief summary of matters discussed, including any action points arising out of the discussion. Simple bullet points are usually easiest for a non-English speaker to follow.

If your native speaker is going to be on your school staff for some months, follow up the initial observation period with a joint evaluation session between mentor, native speaker and a member of the senior management team to review positive aspects of the placement so far, as well as areas for development and targets for improvement, if appropriate.

Where there is only limited foreign language expertise in the host school, both native speakers and class teachers need the support of a specialist in a position to give guidance on the preparation of materials and share techniques appropriate to teaching the foreign language to young learners. Time and personnel permitting, a review visit by an AST, adviser, secondary MFL teacher or project co-ordinator mid-way during a placement can be helpful in checking that all is going well, offering advice and reassurance and ironing out incipient problems.

With the exception of very short appointments, further observation and reflection on primary lessons at intervals during the placement are likely to be valuable and may even be required in those cases where native speakers are student teachers in their countries of origin.

ONGOING OUT-OF-SCHOOL SUPPORT

Whatever the duration of the native speaker's period in your school, it is vital to ensure that full support is given. In Liverpool, the LEA is:

- involved in teaching decisions through distribution of the scheme of work to the SEO (Senior Education Officer) and through regular observation and meetings to keep in touch;
- kept in the loop for communication – the LEA is aware of any assistants and clearance is sought before they work with the children.

The LEA is also able to send native speaker assistants on courses, help with training and give close mentoring. A training programme might involve the observation of primary lessons, intensive training days on primary languages methodology, observation of advisory teachers, with whom the assistants later work, delivering primary languages lessons, team teaching, and ongoing training throughout the year. It might include weekly planning meetings and termly training days. It is also very useful for assistants to have a means of exchanging information, insights and experiences. Observing good practice can be very helpful and motivating.

Where the LEA is in a position to do so, an efficient use of time is for native speakers *and* class teachers to participate in *joint* INSET sessions, with topics relevant to both, rather than for the LEA to lay on separate provision. Some schools are now trying out combined INSET sessions with primary and secondary MFL teachers together.

REVIEW MEETINGS

If you are working in partnership with a higher education institution, the tutors will be observing the native speakers and coming into school. This is likely to be backed up by a series of review meetings held at the university for all native speaker trainees.

Anita Rowell, of Bradford College, suggests combining the first review meeting with afternoon tea. After the first week in school, Anita holds a social weekend activity, to review progress and identify potential problems to be resolved.

CONTINUING PROFESSIONAL DEVELOPMENT

If your primary school is fortunate enough to be able to participate in sessions held by an Early Language Learning Regional Support Group or is offered other opportunities for professional development, such as training sessions laid on by secondary schools, do not forget to include your native speakers. This is especially important for those from the local community, as they will not necessarily have access to any formal training and will appreciate the chance to join in with INSET related to primary languages.

> **! tip** **Ensure that local native speaker assistants have been invited, as the CPD sessions may be offered on days when they are not normally in school and they may be left out unintentionally.**

In Kingswood, South Gloucestershire, primary languages have been extremely well supported through the International Learning and Research Centre. A month's placement in local primary schools is arranged for French trainee teachers from the IUFM (Orléans-Tours). These teachers experience one day a week professional development facilitated by the Head of the ILRC, by a headteacher researcher and by an experienced primary AST. Seminar topics for French native speakers include:

- primary methodology in foreign language teaching;
- the National Curriculum;
- The National Literacy Strategy;
- similarities and differences between primary schools in the UK and France.

At St Bede's School, Lanchester, a primary languages lead teacher from the Specialist Language College is currently delivering the primary languages curriculum with support from class teachers. As she travels round all primary schools each week, this teacher has been able to check up relatively easily and regularly that all is going well and deal with issues as they arise. Liaison and good communication are essential.

Foreign Language Assistants need a base, which can serve as an anchor, where they can be established as a team and where they can share ideas and resources.

Where several native speaker assistants are deployed, it can prove more effective to bring them together as a group rather than to repeat a similar conversation with different individuals on successive occasions. In Richmond upon Thames, the LEA holds timetabled sessions at the Curriculum and Teachers' Centre, usually at the same time each week, thus providing a venue for native speakers to meet together, both informally and for training purposes. The provision of a regular support slot is especially important for assistants at primary school, who generally work in a more isolated and peripatetic capacity.

SOCIAL AND PROFESSIONAL CONTACTS

Check up to see if your native speaker is part of a larger group – if they are a teacher trainee from abroad they are likely to have come across to England in a group, which can serve as a support system for the shyer ones, particularly if they are resident on campus. Others, however, may have come on their own and may feel quite lonely during the initial period in your school, when they are less confident in their spoken English. For some assistants, it may be the first occasion that they have been away from home for an extended period of time. The mentor can help by:

- offering suggestions for social activities, from clubs to churches and arranging for the native speaker to meet other young adults, particularly during the first couple of weeks;
- putting them in contact with other assistants, including those in secondary schools, so that they can socialise and share teaching ideas;
- inviting them to school social events.

Many native speakers, including those permanently resident in this country, really appreciate invitations to teachers' homes or the opportunity to join school outings. St Bede's Specialist Language College states:

> *We have strongly encouraged all primaries to make native speakers feel part of the wider school community. Activities have included staff nights out, invitations to dinner in staff homes, organisation of trips such as football matches, salsa dancing, museums and linked visits to University of Durham School of Education day trips.*

REGIONAL SUPPORT GROUPS

The mentor can further support native speaker assistants by putting the native speakers in touch with other language professionals, especially Early Language Learning Regional Support Groups organised by CILT, the National Centre for Languages (see the NACELL website for a list). These offer five twilight sessions free of charge to any one involved in early language learning and are a source of networking, training and inspiration. Ann Brooks, Headteacher of a nursery and first school in Hampshire, who has an untrained native speaker, Sophie, from the local community working with her, advises accompanying them where possible to local RSG sessions.

In the case below a native speaker from within the local community is being supported to make a valuable contribution to the **whole** life of the school. Note how Ann, the headteacher, and Sophie, the French National, have **worked together** to introduce languages successfully in their school, and how Ann **and** Sophie both participate in the flourishing meetings of the local Early Language Learning Regional Support Group. This means that Ann knows what training and support Sophie is able to access and can feed in suggestions to the co-ordinator to help ensure that sessions meet the needs of teachers in early years and foundation settings. Ann explains:

> *Sophie, a French native speaker from Bordeaux and a graduate in Law, is working with children aged 4–7 at St Michael and All Angels Infant School. She came to the village with her husband, who had come to work in England, and a family of three young boys. Sophie spoke very little English and her two children of school age, when they arrived in*

Years R and 2 had no English at all. As Headteacher, I made a determined effort to support her and welcome the family in accordance with the ethos of our school.

Fortunately, Sophie is a natural communicator and highly intelligent, and soon began to make herself understood in English and became an active participant in our school community. There had already been some French taught in Year 2 by a colleague who was promoted elsewhere just before Sophie arrived and Sophie offered to take over this teaching. We decided to extend the teaching of French to all classes.

In the classes, which last 15–20 minutes, Sophie only uses French. She plays games with the children and teaches them French songs. Last Christmas, Sophie taught the whole school a French Christmas carol, which we sang in church along with an Italian and a Philippino carol. Sophie's husband, Jean-François, read one of the lessons in French and we also had readings in Italian and Philippino. These activities are integrating awareness of other languages into our curriculum and they have been very successful. The children who began in Year R have an ear for the French language, see it as a natural means of communication and speak it without a noticeable English accent. They really enjoy the lessons and they have broadened their linguistic and cultural horizons. This year Sophie has started to give a French lesson to the teaching staff and some Learning Support Assistants on Wednesday lunchtimes and this further enhances the linguistic and cultural awareness in the school.

Sophie and I believe very strongly that the best time to acquire a new language is when children are very young (her own boys are now completely bilingual). We have joined the RSG meetings at Southampton which have given us further support and new ideas.

Finally, further help is also offered by the Association for Language Learning, which is especially keen to support local primary languages and also secondary teachers doing outreach work with families of primary schools. Increasingly, local ALL branches are including events for primary languages teachers (for further information see p87).

Put the native speaker in touch with Advanced Skills Teachers or advisory teachers. They will already be part of a network of professional contacts and a source of local information related to primary languages teaching.

Check whether your LEA is offering any in-service training in primary languages which assistants might attend.

Some institutions ask their trainees to provide a brief report on their placement. An example is included below.

**Primary School Placements 2004 for newly qualified teachers from France
Reflections on your placement**

You are asked to write a brief report, no more than two sides long, in English, about your school experience.

Some ideas to help you:

- Type of school: e.g. age range; number of boys and girls on roll; number and range of languages spoken by the pupils.
- Organisation: e.g. special teaching arrangements; resources; timetable; play and lunchtime arrangements.
- Staffing structure: e.g. number of teachers; number and role of other adults.
- The school's educational philosophy: e.g. aims, values and rules.
- Classroom management: e.g. rewards and sanctions.

You may also wish to investigate areas of personal interest and also to make some comparisons with schools in France.

• • • • •

Taking just some of the above steps to support your native speaker assistant will help ensure that their time in your school is rewarding for everyone. Clearly it is important to give native speakers opportunities to teach which are beneficial to the class teacher but which also give a range of worthwhile experiences and a chance for the native speaker assistant to really contribute. The next chapter presents practical examples of ways in which native speakers have been used effectively in primary schools.

7. Working together with the native speaker assistant

ACTIVITIES AND PROJECTS

The increasing opportunities for children to learn languages from an early age are exciting. The discovery and development of a new communication skill brings enjoyment and enhanced self-esteem. As we prepare for entitlement in 2010, the successful integration of languages into the primary curriculum is being carried out in a variety of contexts and there are many different effective models of delivery (see the NACELL 'Curricular models' document at **www.nacell.org.uk/bestpractice/models.htm** and the 'See a school' section for further practical information). As earlier chapters have indicated, native speaker assistants can, depending on their role, assist with language-based activities, add to the development of social and cultural awareness, or work in a cross-curricular capacity using English. They can also help develop children's creative, physical and social skills. This chapter sums up a number of ways in which native speaker assistants are currently being deployed to support primary languages.

To start with, of course, it is vital, as the previous chapter has suggested, to ensure that your native speaker is supported in his or her planning and also has a chance to work in the way that builds on his or her skills and wishes. Richard Smith from Trafalgar Junior School in Richmond upon Thames advises:

Although you will want the native speaker to support delivery of your scheme of work, do remain flexible so that you can build on the native speaker's particular interests and strengths.

Delphine, our Foreign Language Assistant, worked in two year groups in each of the blocks. In negotiation with me (as Deputy Head and Languages Co-ordinator) and with the class teachers and with Delphine, we discussed what topics and what areas she preferred and whether there were things she felt strongly she wanted to do. We also discussed whether music or singing were her forte. We always make a point of asking about the native speaker's preferred way of working.

Christine, a French Comenius Assistant who team taught with an advisory teacher, says:

> *Before each lesson we would draw up a written lesson plan, so that we could have a clear idea about which of us was to do what. This was convenient for my record keeping [see Chapter 8] and for bearing in mind our objectives.*

 When looking over lesson plans with the native speaker, check that they know how any relevant equipment works, for example a CD or cassette player, OHP, video or photocopier.

Your native speaker may be willing to work additional hours by arrangement. However, it is important not to regard all the additional hours as pupil contact time. Instead, build in specified times for planning and the use of reprographic equipment, for example, to ensure assistants come to sessions well prepared. This will be appreciated, as the following comment by one headteacher suggests: 'The class teachers (receiving the assistant) would have liked a plan, albeit a simple one, of what the children were going to do'.

In the sections below, we offer some examples of ways in which native speaker assistants have contributed to primary languages. Please note that although we have listed suggestions under separate headings, such as language learning, intercultural understanding and cross-curricular links, in practice there will be overlap between the areas.

SUPPORTING LANGUAGE LEARNING ACTIVITIES

The following examples show how native speaker assistants can support language learning activities. For example, Andrew Portas from Hampshire has deployed a Foreign Language Assistant to support the primary languages work currently being delivered via secondary specialists and primary class teachers in feeder primaries. He says:

> *Each class gets one 30-minute teaching input slot per week by a secondary MFL specialist in Year 4 and by the primary teachers in Year 3 (they watched and participated last year when the secondary colleagues were working in Year 3). The Foreign Language Assistant is used to provide more intensive oral practice in small groups of approximately five pupils, of the vocabulary and structures taught by the teacher.*

Elsewhere, Nigel Pearson from Liverpool sums up some of the activities carried out by native speakers in his local education authority, where there is a substantial level of support and where assistants work, as in the above example from Hampshire, alongside specialist teachers. (Nigel can seen working with a German assistant in the CILT Early Language Learning video 3.)

In this model, native speakers:

- teach vocabulary and phrases;
- lead conversations;
- sing songs;
- in **conversations with a specialist language teacher**, offer real live listening experiences;
- help to demonstrate and supervise language games;
- can work with goups of children for activities in the same room as the teacher and cater for specific needs;
- offer authentic accounts of special events in the country of which the language is being taught, concerning festivals and regions;
- provide the children with another voice to which they can listen;
- help to narrate stories, by taking parts.

Also, representatives from commerce and industry (not always native speakers) make occasional visits to schools and, while they may speak in English, they demonstrate the use of languages for the future in the wider world. This can be very motivating.

The following sections provide examples of topics and activities successfully undertaken by native speaker assistants. Again, teachers will need to select those which fit in with their own school's scheme of work, aims and objectives and teaching resources.

TOPIC AREAS

As a starting point, the non-statutory schemes of work for French, German and Spanish at Key Stage 2, published by the Qualifications and Curriculum Authority in 2000, suggest a number of topic areas to act as a framework of language content. Evidence from questionnaires and reports by a large number of native speaker assistants working in a variety of schools and with age groups from Nursery through to Year 6, indicate that they are typically involved in teaching many of the themes which appear in the schemes of work for Key Stage 2. These include:

- greetings and saying goodbye;
- talking about myself (name, age, birthday, likes, dislikes, how I feel);
- talking about my family (brothers and sisters, pets, where we live);
- colours;
- numbers;
- the alphabet;
- contents of a pencil case;
- body parts;
- days of the week;
- months;
- weather;
- telling the time;
- clothes;
- school subjects;
- daily routine;

- food and drink;
- making purchases/handling a different currency.

In addition, a few native speakers report that they have included wild animals or mini-beasts linked with story telling or Science projects.

Of course, there is plenty of scope for you to develop topics and activities according to the needs and interests of your particular pupils.

POPULAR ACTIVITIES

Assistants report that popular activities which have worked well, include:

- game-like activities with flashcards such as *pouce*/heads down, thumbs up;
- games such as 'Noughts and crosses', 'Simon says', lotto, 'Hangman';
- matching pairs with vocabulary and picture cards;
- songs;
- storytelling;
- reading Big Books;
- cooking (and eating) following authentic recipes;
- colouring, drawing, labelling in the target language;
- crossword puzzles;
- worksheets including lots of pictures to support the text.

The above examples indicate that in the early stages, the main **skills** developed are likely to be oracy skills, especially those of:

- listening and responding, (to the native speaker and class teacher/or audio/video cassettes and CD-ROMs, also to simple stories, finger rhymes and songs);
- speaking;
- talking to each other;
- singing.

As children engage in a whole range of activities with their languages teacher and the native speaker, they are of course also developing their **social and interpersonal skills**.

So, for example, children can practise speaking for a real purpose with a native speaker. In Richmond upon Thames, children can be prepared for the Lingua Badge Award. At Trafalgar Junior School, one of the teacher trainees from Créteil was based in Year 6 and as well as working alongside the class teachers, she was involved in preparing them in small groups for their Bronze Lingua Badge Award.

LITERACY

Gradually, once children can confidently and accurately pronounce familiar words, phrases and sentences, the skills of reading and writing can be incorporated, beginning with an awareness of familiar words in written form. At the same time, children will be reinforcing their understanding of their own language(s). As stated earlier, skills are unlikely to be encountered discretely and will often be combined.

Below is a description of work carried out by Isabelle, a French assistant who worked in a nursery school.

Types of activities	Year Groups
Initially Isabella became familiar with the routine of the nursery and got to know the children in the whole nursery setting. At these times she would introduce French words in the context of their everyday play. Then with a group of 12 older children, Isabella developed the current topic of myself - growth, firstly through the theme of birthdays with the intention of 'pulling it all together' and reading a story about a cat and finishing with a video of L'anniversaire de Spot. Her lessons developed from – introducing Spot the dog soft toy + greetings – colours of birthday balloons game – counting game with birthday candles and invitations – positional language using a box and small toy. – names of fruits using real fruit - j'aime - je n'aime pas – animals grande/petite/moyenne.	

ENHANCING INTERCULTURAL UNDERSTANDING

The fourth strand of the Key Stage 2 Framework for MFL is that of intercultural understanding and contact. Working together with a native speaker can help link language work with the culture of the countries in which it is spoken, helping children to begin to recognise and respect each other.

The following examples show how a variety of native speakers in different roles can promote and enhance intercultural understanding.

Yasemin, a Comenius Assistant from Germany, worked in a South-West London LEA. Her role is outlined below.

Tasks:
- to raise awareness of German life and culture;
- to introduce the teaching of German in primary schools;
- to produce materials of long-lasting benefit.

Yasemin

Materials produced:
- photo packs showing aspects of life in Germany, e.g. shops and services, transport, with questions and discussion points related to the National Curriculum for Design and Technology;
- story packs, e.g. *The Pied Piper of Hamelin* and *Goldilocks;*
- German language materials *'Deutsch ist ein Kinderspiel'* for future use.

Number of hours worked:
- fifteen per week, broken down approximately over the year into 90 hours' language teaching, 90 hours' cultural input, 90 hours' planning and preparation.

Activities:
Yasemin led sessions with pupils on:
- schools in Germany;
- German Christmas;
- German cooking;
- Easter in Germany;
- life in Germany;
- German language teaching;
- establishing links with the German School in London;
- establishing links with the twin town;
- help with one school's Comenius project;
- hosting a German lunch for invited guests at the beginning of the placement.

Gains to pupils' knowledge:

- awareness of life in Germany (such as food and festivals) was enhanced through discrete lessons and links with German schools;
- they benefited from an introduction to the language by a native German speaker;
- one school had a 'German week', and this enabled pupils to increase their understanding of the language and culture through cross-curricular projects.

 Sometimes it is tempting to focus on the differences in day-to-day habits and customs. It is, however, important to emphasise similarities that exist between different countries and discuss the things the children have in common.

Other native speakers report that cultural topics linked to their native countries have included:

- land and climate;
- aspects of everyday life at home;
- shopping in the home country;
- food;
- a land of wine;
- fashion and design;
- life in the country and in the city;
- sports and leisure;
- artists and painters;
- famous people;
- famous buildings and landmarks;
- wildlife.

The following example is of how Doris, from Quebec, supported primary languages work in a London primary school.

- Doris first of all introduced herself to each Year 6 class and told them about herself and Quebec.
- The children then worked in six groups. Each week, Doris would work with three of the groups.
- There was a two-week programme.
- Work was set on the body, colours, sports, days of the week and months of the year.
- Children worked on a monster, which they presented to the class in the final session.

Jo Cole, from South Gloucestershire, receives native speaker teacher trainees for four weeks each November. The native speakers' work is linked to the schools' own policy for Early Foreign Language Learning and their scheme of work. They:

- give an introductory lesson about their region of France, showing a map and photos of their family, village/town, special places and Paris and famous sites there;
- tell stories in French to all age groups from Reception to Year 6;
- play games in French that French children play such as *'Un, deux, trois, soleil'* and *'Jacques a dit'*;
- help the class teacher introduce words, phrases and sentences for classroom instructions and activities;

- play numeracy games/do mental maths starter in French part of the numeracy hour;
- help children follow a recipe in French (which links with work on instructional texts in literacy);
- teach a song or rhyme linked to Christmas (as the placement is in November) and make a Christmas card in French.

Sandra, a French native speaker, who worked in two primary schools in Hampshire describes her work on a Christmas theme:

On Tuesday I spoke about Christmas and the pupils learned a French song 'Vive le vent' and made Christmas cards. On Thursday I was in charge of a group of six children and we did Christmas decorations.

The following quote illustrates how a Foreign Language Assistant, shared between a secondary Technology College and several local primary schools prepared joint sessions to teach children about Easter customs in France and *les cloches de Pâques.* Jo Biddle, the secondary AST for MFL who worked with the Foreign Language Assistant, Laurent, team teaching with him in the classroom, describes how this worked.

We had recently received cards from our French friends and wanted to send them a card for Easter. As one of our traditions is that of the Easter hunt and the Easter bunny, we made cards in the shape of a rabbit and learned how to wish the children 'Happy Easter' in French. We then had an Easter hunt, with Laurent giving the instructions as to how warm we were, using expressions that were familiar from teaching the weather, e.g. tu gèles. Using the OHP, Laurent then talked about the tradition of the bells not ringing in the churches before Easter, as they have all flown to Rome to collect the eggs to be dropped over France on Easter Sunday, and he showed a map to illustrate the eggs being dropped.

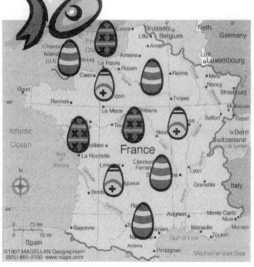

At Christmas the children were able to find out about similarities and differences between the two cultures.

> We first spent some time looking at traditions we have in our own homes, using a little worksheet. The children decided whether the expressions were true or false and we then listened to Laurent give his account of traditions in France, carefully mirroring the kinds of things the children had been thinking about, for example, typical food and Father Christmas. We then turned this into a vrai/faux activity. We made statements about either France or England and the children had to vote by showing their vrai or faux cards in response. We sent some of the worksheets to France to tell the primary school there about our main traditions.

This cultural work was carried on after Christmas on 6 January. Below Laurent describes the way he was able to use school assembly times to introduce junior-aged children to the way in which Epiphany is celebrated in France. He says:

> I did some assemblies in January in two junior schools to celebrate the Fête des rois. The teachers had cooked some Galettes des rois (you can find the recipe very easily on the Web) and we gathered the children to eat it according to French traditions. The youngest child sits down under the table on which the galette is. An adult cuts a piece of the cake and asks, Pour qui celle-la? (who's this one for?). The child answers with a name. In the cake there is a fève – a little character, or piece of something or a dry bean. The child who finds the fève when they eat their cake becomes the king or queen of the day and has to choose his or her king or queen. The teachers had prepared two paper crowns to place on the heads of the royal couple. The children were really happy doing this and those who were allergic to nuts (there are almonds in the pastry) were usually chosen as the kings and queens.

CROSS-CURRICULAR LINKS

Opposite is an extract from a lesson plan on a Japanese wave painting which a trainee from France devised for Key Stage 1 children. The children acted out the movement of the waves in the painting, then compared it to a painting of tranquil water by Monet and did their own pictures in various styles as well as using lots of adjectives to describe the sea.

Lesson Plan ART → THE STORMY JAPANESE SEA.

Class: KS1	Year Group: 1	School:	Date: 10/3

Lesson (title and summary)	Prior learning
How to make a stormy sea? Uses of the hand.	→ the plain lines (horizontal + vertical). → the curls.

Teaching objectives	Core vocabulary
- To be able to identify ≠ parts of a drawing (missing parts). - To be able to id the movements of the hand needed to draw the ≠ states of the sea.	- The movements of the sea: → outburst → curls = ANIMAL'S CLAWS → withdrawing → loops → expanding → ringlet → bubbles

Resources	
- the original picture - 2 transparents w/ missing parts	- 1 copy w/ the outlines (for ch tests) - black colour pen. A3/A4 sheets.

Introduction	Key structures
① Presentation of the original drawing - id of its characteristics (stormy) - comparison w/ Monet's picture. ② id of the movements: - zigzaging - about to crash over the boat, - bubbling	On the drawing we can see notice identify. Adjectives: → stormy → wild → unleashed → raging
	Time 5/10

Main teaching activities (presentation, practice, production)	Organisation (whole class, groups, resources, role of other adults)
① How did the painter draw the waves, what mvmnt did he made with the hand. ② Use of the overhead projector: Part 1: mvmt from 1 side to the other zigzag. SHOULDER → ← Part 2: mvmt ↑ WRIST + CURLS / PS: Bubbles ③ Practice on a sheet of paper: ≠3 tests 15 min before the last try. Final drawing on a A4 sheet, all the children working on their own.	① Collectively, the children are sitting on the mat. ② Indv / whole class, the children mime the artist's movements of the hand. ③ Indv: The children tries several time to reproduce the movements: at each attempt, they focus on a ≠ part of the sea.
15 → tests / 30 → Final work	Time 45

Plenary (review)	Key questions
→ The teacher shows the different outcome (the instructions are respected or not). followed or not → what was hard to do?	- How did the painter draw the waves? - Can you mime the movement the he has to do to make this part of the wave (≠ ressources) - what was the part you had difficulty with? (details)
	Time 5

Geography and work relating to the study of other countries, weather and the points of the compass also provide opportunities to link languages work with other areas of the primary curriculum. Have a look at the example below, in which Jo Biddle, who supervised Laurent from France, describes how she taught alongside Laurent in the primary classroom to introduce children to major towns and a cultural feature associated with each of them. As Laurent pointed out the towns on the map, Jo drew pictures/symbols to represent each town on the whiteboard.

When teaching a little geography about France it was again very useful to have Laurent to liaise with. We initially decided on six towns that would be interesting to talk about and that covered the whole of France. Laurent and I were able to pick out key facts about each place to make the places more memorable for the pupils and facts that could be represented by a symbol that they could then draw onto a map, e.g. Strasbourg – represented by French and German flags because of the European Parliament; Lille – destination for Eurostar therefore a symbol of the train; Marseille famous for pétanque and the harbour and its walk – symbol of a boat etc. Laurent introduced a story about each of the towns we chose and the pupils were able to remember many of the simple facts we had picked out.

Later this work was combined with work on the weather – *la météo*, complete with *Pierre* the French puppet giving the forecast from behind a chair which served as a pretend television screen.

Jo clarifies:

> *I have used Laurent throughout to provide perfect pronunciation models
> and have been able to model whole dialogues using puppets with us both
> taking roles. Laurent's voice became associated with that of his puppet
> Pierre and the children also enjoyed listening out to a tape I asked him to
> record, where he asked questions on numbers:* 'Où est le numéro dix?',
> *right the way up to 31, calling for numbers at random. The pupils had to
> listen for their number and jump up and shout* ' Ici, Pierre, ici'.

From the above suggestions we can see that foreign language work undertaken by native speakers and class teacher **working together** can help **reinforce skills that children are learning and using in other areas of the primary curriculum**. Examples are:

* literacy and numeracy support via alphabet and number work;
* mental arithmetic, maths starters, class surveys, block graphs, pie charts, dates, 24-hour clock, length, area, shape, size;
* artistic skills: painting, collage, posters, cutting, folding, modelling, mask and puppet making;
* book making: copy writing simple captions and illustrating;
* ball skills: playground games and physical skills;
* physical responses to the native speaker's instructions issued in the target language (with the class teacher present and in charge);
* music and movement;
* ICT skills such as word processing, text manipulation, PowerPoint presentations;
* using e-mail to send and receive messages from e-pals, or partner schools abroad.

SPECIAL EVENTS AND PROJECTS INVOLVING NATIVE SPEAKER ASSISTANTS

Anita Rowell from Bradford College reports that visiting trainees can:

* produce attractive displays about the foreign country either in the classroom or in the **main entrance foyer to the school**;
* put on a French breakfast in school;
* prepare children to perform dialogues and role plays or a drama production or assembly in the foreign language.

Other special projects might include:

* helping run a language club for children;
* preparing special European dishes;
* preparations for a foreign language festival/day/week;
* a *boules* competition;
* a Bastille day;
* helping with a fashion show;
* help with the Christmas play or with songs for harvest or Easter.

The following is an example of an end-of-year celebration. At the end of the summer term, to celebrate a year of French in Upham CE Primary School, Laurent from Paris was involved in putting on a final show for pupils, teachers and parents before his return to France. This involved a small class of Year 3 and 4 pupils, with the specialist MFL teacher and Laurent, the native speaker, orchestrating the show from the left- and right-hand side of the hall. Pierre, the French puppet joined in and, by standing with their backs to the audience, it was possible to hold up flashcards as prompts for the verses of songs to support the children performing. This was a real celebration of all that had been learnt over the whole year, with little role plays and activities which demonstrated what the children had discovered, both linguistically and culturally. Every child participated in a truly inspiring assembly.

Kathleen Manley, head of a Specialist Language College in Medway, gives us a host of illustrations of special projects with which native speakers from a variety of language backgrounds, assisted.

Kathleen Manley

Antonio, a Foreign Language Assistant in Spanish, helped a local primary school on a weekly basis for one term. His brief was to help the headteacher with a lunchtime Spanish club and provide the authentic native speaker dimension. Antonio spent time in preparation for his primary visits discussing content and strategy with me.

Rebecca, a French Foreign Language Assistant, ran a French Club for one term in local primary school.

Martha, an Austrian Overseas Qualified Teacher, taught Italian to Year 2 children as part of a special programme aimed at easing transition between Key Stages 1 and 2. The programme, at Balfour Academy, ended with a performance from each participating group.

Kathleen reports that occasionally they are required to hold special events to celebrate language. Native speakers (Foreign Language Assistants, Graduate Teachers, Overseas Qualified Teachers and Newly Qualified Teachers) participate by preparing authentic foods, and teaching some basic language and traditional games.

Recent events include:

- **Asia Focus Week**: Japanese and Thai native speakers contribute to cultural activities based on the culture of their country.
- **Chinese New Year**: The local Chinese community contributed to Chinese Week by staging a dragon dance in assembly and donating decorations for the hall. The Chinese students in the sixth form of the school organised activities for each lunchtime, such as showing a Chinese film, teaching Chinese, Calligraphy and Chinese games.

- **The European Fayre**: Organised for the benefit of the visiting Japanese students. Foreign Language Assistants prepared authentic foods and taught some basic language and traditional games.

The following example, also from Kathleen Manley, illustrates how native speaker assistants, with support, can **extend** and **challenge** children. Kathleen tells us about the Children's University.

> *The Children's University runs on Saturday mornings every term and lasts a total of four weeks. It is aimed at Year 6 students and is designed to challenge and stretch them. As a Language College, we offer different languages including French, Spanish and Japanese. Russian, German and Thai have also been offered some years.*
>
> *The Foreign Language Assistants and/or Graduate Teachers (CILT) are usually asked to deliver the course, with strong support from myself in terms of training, making resources and, of course, planning the session content. We also have a Japanese native speaker who delivers Children's University.*

Kathleen goes on to indicate the high level of focused support she provides, which is vital for the success of the undertaking:

> *The support I offer consists of weekly meetings to plan the session and give guidance on resources. Occasionally, this means that the Foreign Language Assistant will make OHTs, games and other activities. Further to this specific input, I take them through different activities and games that they will be able to use. We also look at how to pitch the level of teaching and how to make the sessions enjoyable and well-paced, as well as differentiation.*

Other ideas for collaborative work with a native speaker are:

- help in the production of newsletters about European affairs;
- participation in joint language projects with other primary schools, both in the UK and abroad;
- help setting up pen pal/e-mail/exchange links with schools in the country of origin through contacting embassies and tourist offices for up-to-date documentation, telephone calls, translation and exchange of information.

Andy Burford, Head Teacher of Liss Junior, reports that their native speaker was invaluable in helping sort out arrangements for links with partner schools abroad particularly when it came to clarifying arrangements, making telephone contact and prompting responses to the cultural parcels sent to the partner classes.

Andy explains:

> *We arranged for each of the four lower junior classes to make an individual link with schools in France. Initially we used the Windows On The World website to identify partner schools. To speed up communication our native speaker telephoned the contact person in France and discussed our programmes of work. Having established the suitability of the partnership she then explored possible links. Where appropriate it was agreed with the French schools to exchange small gifts/artefacts to stimulate discussion. Two schools sent us examples of French sweets, one sent us details of how they marked April Fool's Day with a poisson d'avril (April fish). We sent each school a jar of Marmite with 'instructions' – sure to stimulate a response!*

HELP FOR TEACHING STAFF AND OTHER ADULTS

Bear in mind that native speakers can also support class teachers and teaching assistants. So for example, in addition to working with the children, Foreign Language Assistants in Surrey compiled and recorded an audio-cassette of classroom language in French, German, Spanish and Italian. A booklet of guidelines published by the County Council included a list of all the target-language expressions which had been recorded, together with their translations. This meant that teachers could select the phrases they wished to use in their primary languages lessons, which they could listen to and practise whenever convenient for them. Similarly, native speaker assistants in South Gloucestershire primary schools have been involved in supporting class teachers from several linked primary schools by putting all the vocabulary on tape from the MFL Key Stage 2 Scheme of work. Each school receives a copy.

Jo Cole from South Gloucestershire explains how accent and pronunciation is improved working with recorded material.

> *The Foreign Language Assistant also helped with the International Learning and Research Centre and CfBT-funded story making project. She taped the French stories children were learning to tell from memory. She worked in the story making project primary schools teaching the children the stories. Their accents were much better because of this – pronunciation was accurate because they had listened so carefully.*

Native speakers can also help deliver a presentation on projects in which they are involved, or teach authentic songs and rhymes at a local Early Language Learning Regional Support Group meeting so that the benefit of having an assistant reaches a wider audience. They can also produce materials for games, which can be demonstrated at teachers' meetings and copied for use in all the participating schools, which both saves time and creates shared experiences for teachers and children in local schools, as Jo Cole points out.

In another local education authority, Susanne, an Austrian Comenius Assistant gives us the following feedback about her work to support primary languages teachers. She says:

> With the French assistants, I helped with two in-service training sessions. We worked in groups with the teachers and helped them to translate some well-known stories into French, German and Spanish. These were made into a booklet and sent out to all of the schools.

In Hampshire, native speakers have been used to run an after-school conversation class as part of a **French club for adults** in the primary school to help improve their confidence and fluency. Sandra, the native speaker, describes how this worked.

> From October to February, I did French conversation with the teachers in the primary school. The topics of conversation were free. Then, from the end of February to the end of March, I did French with a different group of people who were less advanced. I was in charge of reinforcing basic vocabulary. Each week the lesson was dedicated to a different topic.'

Here is what one of the teachers who joined this French club had to say:

> Sandra has been very helpful for the staff as well, working with us to raise our awareness of the language to assist our own teaching. We will miss her very much.

And a teaching assistant adds:

> Sandra has really helped me improve my French. She has been very enthusiastic. I've really enjoyed it. It has helped my confidence when speaking and this will be most useful when I am on the French exchange soon.

In Medway, native speaker assistants linked to a Specialist Language College also assist with **adult language learning in the wider community**. Kathleen Manley, Head of the Specialist Language College explains:

> We offer lessons in MFL to the local adult community (parents, colleagues, older students). Each year, the French, German and Spanish assistants deliver classes in these languages. Again, they are supported by training sessions and consultation meetings to monitor progress, address needs, as well as develop strategies and materials.

FAMILY LEARNING

In Richmond upon Thames, **family learning** takes place after school in some schools. Delphine, one of the French Foreign Language Assistants has been assisting a specialist teacher from La Jolie Ronde in the running of after-school sessions.

And of course, in addition, native speakers can participate in non-foreign language specific events such as going out on trips with children (not just foreign language visits). Richard Smith lists a number of outings, in which one of the teacher trainees from Créteil has taken part:

- going to a local military band concert at Kneller Hall;
- attending a Shakespeare workshop at the Orange Tree Theatre;
- accompanying Year 6 pupils to a children's bookshop where, as school leavers, they are able to choose a book.

These activities are not necessarily to do with teaching French at all, but are enriching for the teacher trainee who intends to teach English on return to France and who is interested in all sorts of aspects of the English education system, including the special activity days available after SATs in the summer term.

● ● ● ● ●

As we have seen, the ways of working with a native speaker assistant are many and varied and will need to be adapted to an individual school's circumstances. This will depend on the extent of language teaching provision and the amount of experience the school has in hosting visiting assistants. In conclusion, the brief analysis from St Richard's with St Andrew's C.E. Primary School in Richmond upon Thames (opposite) shows how languages fit into the primary environment.

From the variety of suggestions and experience reflected in this chapter, it is clear that native speaker assistants can make a valuable contribution to primary languages teaching. As we have seen, it is important for host primary schools to give their native speaker assistants appropriate induction and ongoing support. The assistants are typically in school for a limited period of time and it is essential that assistants 'hit the ground running' and that they and the schools derive maximum benefit from the experience. As teachers, it is worth us remembering that for these assistants coming to us from abroad, this experience can be life changing and it is certainly a unique opportunity for them. It will also be vital to maintain momentum and interest in the native speaker's country of origin. The final chapter suggests how this might be done.

Primary languages in our school	
How long has our school been teaching a language?	*10 years*
Which languages and which year groups?	*French: From Reception up to Year 6, wherever possible!*
Who teaches the foreign language?	*French Co-ordinator, and class teachers in a more limited way, although this is beginning to develop.*
Why did we decide to use a native speaker assistant?	*Very good experience for the children – makes learning a language more real and purposeful. Good experience for teacher – leads to improved delivery.*
How do we obtain native speaker assistants?	*Courtesy of LEA's French assistant scheme; regular participation in hosting French teacher trainees; sharing an assistant from Grey Court Secondary School, as part of their outreach programme.*
Which languages and cultures do our native speakers represent?	*French, German.*
Deployment	
How long are the native speakers with us?	*Varies – there are blocks of visits and this provides a skeleton of opportunity throughout the school.*
How do we support the native speakers?	*We welcome and make them feel part of the staff; explain and offer resources; work alongside; offer point of contact throughout the day; meet socially after school; write a reference for them.*
What are the advantages and benefits to us?	*Modelling; teacher improvement; children's enthusiasm maintained; keeping abreast of language and culture.*
What advice do staff need?	*• Regular monitoring throughout the school day.* *• Allow native speaker assistants to teach in their own style.* *• Through team teaching develop a consistent approach which can be carried on after the native speaker leaves.*
What is the main benefit to pupils?	*Prepares children for types of questions that develop their knowledge of a foreign culture.*

8. Building on the work of the native speaker assistant

MAINTAINING ENTHUSIASM

It is important to build on the input by the native speaker at various different points, and the primary curriculum offers many opportunities for the primary teacher to reinforce elements of the foreign language as part of classroom routines throughout the school day by, for instance:

- greeting, praising and dismissing children – calling the register/getting the class to number off, taking the dinner money;
- lining children up;
- giving basic classroom instructions;
- doing mental arithmetic;
- giving simple instructions in the foreign language in practical subjects such as PE;
- practising songs, poems and rhymes in the foreign language;
- reading a story in the foreign language;
- making craft items with simple foreign language instructions;
- helping pupils create bilingual displays, allowing pupils access to software and websites where they can play with the language.

RECORD KEEPING

As the native speaker will eventually be moving on from your school, it is essential that he or she be encouraged to leave behind a record of his or her work. In order to facilitate progression and continuity, you will need to know what was covered, which resources were used and which children the assistant worked with.

Encourage **all** native speakers to keep records and especially teacher trainees, Foreign Language Assistants and Comenius Assistants who will be working in your school only briefly. They could keep a diary, such as the example opposite kept by Sandra that indicates what she did in each of her lessons at the primary school:

Week 8

Focus: *revise colours*

I distributed a colouring worksheet (a paper with eight spaces to colour in) and I asked the pupils to colour in on their worksheet the colours I called out in the different squares. For instance, I said 'La case un est rouge'. They had to colour the first box in red. I also encouraged each pupil to remember what colour was in each box, by asking for example 'La case deux est de quelle couleur?' and they had to name the colour.

Then, at the end of the lesson, the children listened to a French song about the colours and they had to recognise which colours were mentioned in the song.

Session outlines similar to the above are written in a spiral-bound booklet entitled 'My experience as a French assistant in primary schools.' The same booklet includes the formal A4-size reports by participating teachers, which are sent to the British Council Education and Training Group at the end of the assistant's placement. Children from each year group with whom Sandra worked have also recorded their comments, some of which are included below.

I liked doing songs with you Chris
(Year 3 pupil)

I liked learning Je suis
(Year 3 pupil)

Sandra has really encouraged me to learn French.
(Year 4 pupil)

In total, the quotes from all the pupils offer a level of detail that enables the next assistant to see at a glance the kinds of activities and foreign language that Sandra used and which classes they were used with. This can then inform future planning.

Make sure that:
- **assistants' teaching records are filed somewhere accessible so that anyone who needs them for teaching purposes can use them;**
- **the resources produced by the native speakers are not simply left on a shelf. Catalogue them and make them available for use by future native speaker assistants, so that over the years you gradually build up a useful resources bank. There is little point in subsequent assistants re-inventing the wheel.**

SETTING UP LINKS AND CONTACTS

If you have got on well with your native speaker, it may be possible to continue contact with them and their school abroad via e-mail links, letters and the exchange of shoe boxes containing items representative of the country or place, or artefacts which will bring the language and culture alive. Jo Cole can be seen at the end of ELL video 1 using scrap books received from a partner school abroad to stimulate discussion of celebrations as well as food, toys and items from her Key Stage 1 pupils' everyday lives. One junior school uses the European Day of Languages to involve as many native speakers as possible with an accent on fun, for example flamenco in the school hall, an Italian parent teaching some Italian and a Greek parent some cookery.

Over time, your school can gradually build up an international network and this can be useful if you wish to develop any European-funded initiatives. There is a range of possibilities available via the British Council Education and Training Group, from Teachers' International Professional Development (TIPD) opportunities to Arion Study Visits (for key decision makers), to class-to-class projects. In turn, your native speaker assistants will be able to help you maintain these links by supporting you when communicating with partners abroad. New opportunities arise all the time, so it is best to consult the British Council's website to ensure that you have current information. There is likely to be an officer in your LEA who is the main point of contact locally for the British Council and who might be able to advise you.

Finally, try to ensure that there are more staff than just the mentor who are interested in the international dimension. A lot of good work is lost when only a single member of staff is involved with native speakers – when they leave, a lot of the networking can go with them.

It may also be the case that your native speaker assistant might be interested in training as a primary school teacher by doing a primary PGCE with French, German, Italian, Spanish or Portuguese. You can direct them to up-to-date information via the websites of the Teacher Training Agency or CILT, the National Centre for Languages.

Conclusion

As the languages entitlement in primary schools approaches, there is a growing need for native-speaker input.

As we hope we have demonstrated in this Young Pathfinder, native speakers can make a vital contribution to the work of the primary school, both as regards early foreign language learning and in a variety of other ways. They can enhance children's understanding of their own culture(s) as well as that of others, make links between the teaching of curriculum subjects and languages and become involved in the everyday life of the school, accompanying pupils on outings and extra curricular activities.

Schools would generally agree that well-supported native speaker assistants provide a huge amount of added value to their language teaching, as seen from these comments from the headteacher of a special school in Richmond upon Thames:

> *Pupils were motivated when taught by a French person and really tried hard to speak fluently. On family holidays it was reported that some pupils used the French that they had learnt.*

Nonetheless, untrained assistants helping the primary teacher require substantial support from both a language specialist and a primary practitioner. This should be offered early on and, where possible, be ongoing throughout their period of employment. A scheme of work will help them plan appropriately and, if at all possible, they need to have teaching strategies demonstrated. Even though they are native speakers, assistants are likely to require guidance in their use of the target language as a medium for teaching, particularly as regards presenting new language, setting up and running activities and meeting pupils' comprehension needs. Where these activities are intended to link with the ongoing primary curriculum, close liaison with either the class teacher or Primary Languages co-ordinator is paramount.

In this book, we have offered you a range of ideas and possibilities for obtaining the services of – and deploying – a native speaker assistant. If you are a teacher in a school that has never gone down this route before, we hope that this will have given you encouragement to get started. In order to 'make the case' to your headteacher or governors, you will need to give some thought as to the resources available locally. Is there an LEA adviser who can help you? Is it possible to become part of any initiatives led by your local higher education institution? Do you know of any native speakers within the local community who might be interested to work with you? Depending on which type of scheme you decide to use, you will need to check out requirements such as cost implications, whether you would have to find somewhere for the assistant to live and deadlines for any applications. If you are contemplating getting a native speaker assistant for the first time to enhance your languages work in primary school, the reference list at the end of this book gives further sources of support.

As we have seen, whenever native speakers become fully integrated in primary school life, their work has an impact far beyond the contact time allocated to foreign language sessions. Successful and well-supported native speakers leave behind a positive outlook towards other parts of the world, with teachers eager to repeat the experience of collaborating with a native speaker and children looking forward to meeting another 'real' foreign person. Joint preparation and planning and adequate support are the key to success!

> *The year as an assistant is a super experience on a linguistic, professional and cultural level. It is a year that passes very quickly. Make the most of it! (Audrey, Guadeloupe)*

References

CILT (2001) *Early Language Learning video 1: Making it happen.* CILT.

CILT (2002) *Early Language Learning video 2: Making it work.* CILT.

CILT (2003) *Early Language Learning video 3: Making it better.* CILT.

DfES (2002) *National Languages Strategy: Languages for all, Languages for life.* DfES.

National Association of Head Teachers (1992) Resolution: *Modern Foreign Languages in the primary school.* NAHT.

Nuffield Foundation (2000) *Languages, the next generation.* Nuffield Foundation.

Satchwell, P. (1997) Young Pathfinder 5: *Keep talking: Teaching in the target language.* CILT.

Useful sources of information

General

Association for Language Learning: **www.all-languages.org.uk**.

British Council Education and Training Group: **www.britishcouncil.org.uk**.

CILT, the National Centre for Languages: **www.cilt.org.uk**.

'Foreign Language Assistants: Notes for schools and colleges and language assistants': available from the British Council Education and Training Group, 10 Spring Gardens, London SW1A 2BN. E-mail: **assistants@britishcouncil.org**.

National Advisory Centre on Early Language Learning: **www.nacell.org.uk**.

Qualifications, Curriculum and Assessment Authority: **www.qca.org.uk**.

Teacher Training Agency: **www.tta.gov.uk**.

French

Early Start French 1: *Salut. Ça va?* and Early Start French 2: *Où habites-tu?* Kilbery, I. and Rowe, I. Early Start Languages. Website: **www.earlystart.co.uk**.

Quelques renseignements à l'intention des Assistants Français au Royaume Uni and *La boite à outils de l'Assistant de Français au Royaume Uni* are available from the French Embassy. Website: **www.francealacarte.org.uk/assistants**.

Pilote moi (2001) and *Pilote mon école* (2003): interactive CD-ROM. Kent Educational Television (KETV). Website: **www.ketv.co.uk**.

GERMAN

3, 2, 1 los video-based packs for primary German. Early Start Languages.

STEPS: a website with practical information and advice for German Language Assistants, prepared by the Goethe-Institut at **www.goethe.de/gr/lon/steps/index.htm**.

SPANISH

Early Start Spanish. Early Start Languages.

Guia para auxiliares de conversación en el Reino Unido and *Actividades para la clase de Español* ('Guide for conversation assistants' and 'Activities for Spanish classes') are available from the Consejería de Educación y Ciencia at the Spanish Embassy: **www.cec.spain-org.uk**.